Connecting Character to Conduct

Helping Students Do the Right Things

Rita Stein • Roberta Richin • Richard Banyon
• Francine Banyon • Marc Stein

Association for Supervision and Curriculum Development
Alexandria, VA USA

Association for Supervision and Curriculum Development
1703 N. Beauregard St. • Alexandria, VA 22311-1714 USA
Telephone: 1-800-933-2723 or 703-578-9600 • Fax: 703-575-5400
Web site: http://www.ascd.org • E-mail: member@ascd.org

Printed in the United States of America.

ASCD Product No. 100209

s10/2000

ASCD member price: $18.95   nonmember price: $22.95

Library of Congress Cataloging-in-Publication Data
Connecting character to conduct : helping students do the right things /
Rita Prager Stein ... [et al.].
     p. cm.
Includes bibliographical references and index.
"ASCD Product No. 100209"—T.p. verso.
   ISBN 0-87120-388-X (alk. paper)
   1. Character—Study and teaching—United States.   2. Students—United
States—Conduct of life.   3. Curriculum planning—United States.   I.
Stein, Rita Prager, 1945–
   LC311 .C63 2000
   371.8—dc21   00-010589

06 05 04 03 02 01 00   10 9 8 7 6 5 4 3 2 1

Marc Stein paced while he listened to us express what we wanted to accomplish and contribute through this book. After each of us had spoken, Marc said, "So what you're actually proposing is an approach to transforming the normative structure of the school, so everyone learns and stays safe." In that one sentence, Marc articulated our shared purpose. He used his imagination, intellect, and heart to find a shared framework for our individual contributions. Just one month later, on the day our proposal for this book was complete, Marc Stein's gentle heart stopped beating. In the first stunned and grief-filled weeks, Marc was mourned within and well beyond our small group. The loss of this well-loved husband, father, brother, lifelong friend, esteemed colleague, and new coauthor remains palpable. Marc's presence as an irrepressible, deeply respected member of our team is felt on each page. We dedicate this book and our work to his life and his memory.

CONNECTING CHARACTER TO CONDUCT
Helping Students Do the Right Things

Acknowledgments

We thank the many educators, children, and parents who helped us refine our character and conduct approach to education. We are especially grateful for the support and encouragement of the teachers and administrators who carefully read our work, tested our hypotheses, and gave us feedback. We are indebted to the Deer Park Union Free School District Board of Education and Superintendent Don Bright, and to the Half Hollow Hills Central School District Board of Education and Superintendent Kevin N. McGuire. Through the efforts of many people, schools in those districts have incorporated our character and conduct approach to education into their comprehensive educational programs. Using the program shows their commitment to creating school communities where all children can excel and be safe. Deer Park professional staff and Teacher Association President Lyn Warner and Half Hollow Hills professional staff and Teacher Association President Richard Lee gave us crucial guidance and support throughout our writing and pilot program process.

We thank James Borland at Columbia University Teacher's College for his academic support for the research on decision making. We appreciate the efforts of Harvey Stedman, Joanne Stedman, and the faculty at New York University for encouraging us to pursue our circle of character and conduct approach to teaching and learning and for showcasing our work.

We remain thankful to our families and friends for their love and their constant support. Eve and Irving Richin inspired our love for the written word. Our children, Norell, Jarrett, Alexis, Matthew, Erica, and Lauren, and our sisters, Barbara, Linda, and Laurette, have missed us and emotionally supported us as we labored to create our character and conduct approach. Best of all, they handled our repeated absences with respect, impulse control, compassion, and equity.

Special thanks go to Jarrett Stein for his invaluable role in developing Chapter 5: Play Ball. He contributed insight from his experiences as an athlete from Little League to Division I baseball. He also contributed the knowledge he has accrued as a school psychologist, a school administrator, and a workshop facilitator. Jarrett helped us understand the intrinsic connection between character and athletics.

We are grateful to one another for making our individual dreams a reality. Who would have guessed that technology and our own indomitable drive could help us reach our collective crystallizing moment? Last, but never least, we thank our editor, Mark Goldberg, for his wisdom, good nature, irrepressible sense of humor, and gentle corrections. This book would not have been possible without his guidance and the special touch of our favorite waitress who served us during our meetings with Mark.

Introduction

This book started the same way our collaborative work started: by asking middle school students to describe the most difficult decision they ever had to make. Our format was varied, mostly formal interviews and journal writing exercises. We were entirely unprepared for what they shared with us. They helped us understand that, though they were struggling with all the predictable adolescent concerns about homework and what to wear, they were also deciding which parent to live with, which religion to observe, or whether to keep a secret about a friend's thoughts of suicide.

Our students helped us understand that they are making life-altering, long-term decisions with short-term reasoning skills, insufficient adult guidance, and no core frame of reference for making the right decisions for the right reasons in contemporary society. At the same time, they are under great pressure to learn academic content and get good grades. Children are making life-changing decisions—often alone, often for the wrong reasons, often with enduring, negative results. These negative results ripple until they widen to affect families, schools, and communities. Our interviews and personal research consistently revealed that students, from the most affluent to the most impoverished, are making decisions about how to deal with

• Divorce, parental dating, remarriage, changing family structures, and family living arrangements that disrupt the continuity and stability of their personal and academic life
• Persistent feelings of being alone and anonymous in the midst of their own schools, neighborhoods, and homes
• Hundreds of hours alone or with their friends, with no adult supervision or guidance
• Addictions and depression
• Feelings of being left out

1

- Fear of other kids, teachers, and other adults
- Concerns about whether they will live to adulthood

Not one child named an important decision that addressed academic learning or school conduct. Not one child named a decision that reflected evidence of healthy moral development. Not one child named a decision that was made on the basis of a clear, proven method for decision making or problem solving. In fact, each child reported more negative than positive consequences of his decisions.

Clearly, we needed to analyze what we learned from our students and to determine how we would use that information to help all members of school communities teach our children the knowledge, attitudes, and skills they need to live well and learn well in today's increasingly complex world. Only after we carefully examined what we had learned from dozens of similar experiences in the classroom could we decide what we would accomplish.

What Did We Learn from Our Students?

From their journal responses and interview answers, we learned that many of our children are

- Making sophisticated decisions alone˙
- Living solitary lives
- Making important decisions alone, on the basis of peer input or guidance from media (ranging from TV to the Internet)
- Using short-term thinking to make long-term decisions
- Acting out violently and hurting themselves and others
- Lacking basic academic skills, social skills, or both
- Conducting themselves inappropriately, especially under the ordinary, everyday pressures of school life
- Reporting that parents, teachers, and other adults in their lives know little, if anything, about the things they worry about and act on every day

When we shared our results with educators and parents, their responses matched our own. They were highly motivated to discover a practical, positive approach to help all students make sound decisions now and in the future. The educators and parents we spoke with were equally motivated to ensure that such an approach fit naturally into the everyday goals, objectives, and routines typical of our public schools.

Reaching into our varied experiences as classroom teachers, administrators, counselors, and psychologists, we knew that

- Schools have an extraordinary opportunity to help students make the right decisions for the right reasons
- Schools are uniquely equipped to engage parents and other stakeholders in helping students use guiding, universal principles for individual and group decision making
- Schools are not using their influence in ways that significantly and measurably affect how our students make decisions and solve problems
- Our students feel pressured to make the right decisions in school and in the rest of their lives—and they don't know how

It was clear that add-on programs could not offer today's students sufficiently sustained, meaningful learning opportunities. Just as we all know that children reach academic benchmarks when we give them sufficient time and natural opportunities to construct and use their knowledge and skills, we all know that students need the same time and opportunity to develop character and conduct.

We also know that we can help children develop character and conduct through our academic programs. We already offer an academic program to help our students listen, speak, read, and write. We also encourage students to engage in conduct that demonstrates respect, impulse control, compassion, and equity. We can help students succeed in these academic and conduct areas when we use the guiding principles to align our teaching, counseling, and discipline practices. As a result, our children can meet and share our aspirations across the grade levels.

How Can Schools Do Better?

We can begin to help our students cope by approaching our schools as we would approach any powerful, successful system that embraces and supports all its members (Senge, 1998). All such systems have four essential elements that everyone in the system understands:

- The purposes of that system
- The members of that system
- The roles assigned each member to achieve individual and systemwide purposes
- The rules, or guiding principles and practices, that members follow to fulfill their roles and achieve individual and systemwide purposes

We can commit to using what we know about human development as we learn to teach all our children how to conduct themselves (Damon, 1998; Kohlberg, 1981). We can abandon approaches to teaching character and conduct that are add-ons, special courses, one-day programs, or other special events because such simplistic approaches lead us to superficially "cover the curriculum." We can follow the advice of Jacobs (1998) and ask ourselves, "What is in the best interests of my students? What curriculum elements shall [I] select to meet their needs?"

We can clearly state the guiding principles and practices of character and conduct that will help our schools achieve their purposes and make those principles and practices the foundation for our daily operations (Keeney, 1994). We can specifically teach our students to use these guiding principles to make good decisions every day

(Goleman, 1997; Gardner, 1991). We can methodically integrate these guiding principles into the existing curriculums, discipline programs, counseling services, and entire normative structure of the school (Jacobs, 1998, 1999).

We can engage parents and other community stakeholders in partnerships to support the principles of character and conduct that help our children make good decisions. We can use the guiding principles of character and conduct to make our school communities safer, better disciplined, and more welcoming places to learn and work.

Guiding Principles and Practices to Help Schools Do Better

Schools are systems that share a common purpose: to help all children learn well. The members of the system, from the board of education to the students to the bus drivers, have specific and interdependent roles to play. The system will be most successful in achieving its purpose when each member follows four guiding principles, easily remembered with the acronym RICE:

• **Respect:** Show respect toward ourselves and others. Avoid violating or interfering with boundaries. Remember these key ideas: The words we use and the actions we choose show how we feel about ourselves. The way we treat people, animals, and objects shows our respect for ourselves.

• **Impulse control:** Do the right things for the right reasons automatically, even under stress. Do anything else in our imagination. Make sure that we have at least two ways in and out of any situation.

• **Compassion:** Find things in common with other people, even when they seem very different, to develop empathy and to remind us that everyone and everything deserves respect and care.

• **Equity:** Allow everyone to get what she needs to succeed. Remember that each of us is equally and differently equipped to succeed. Treat everyone with fairness.

All of these principles are connected to moral development, language arts, systems, citizenship, and discipline. As such, they are already part of every standards-driven curriculum and instructional program. Our experience supports that all schools can use existing resources, structures, and strengths to help diverse students make the right decisions for the right reasons and to create positive influences that extend well beyond school walls. We have taught the four guiding principles in workshops in New York, Rhode Island, and Pennsylvania. The principles are also used in many New York schools. To sharpen the focus of this book, we have created composite scenarios and examples. When we do our work in local schools, we often represent the concept as the circle of character and conduct because we view it as having drawn a circle around the daily life of schools and tried to infuse character and conduct education into every aspect of school life.

Although the Centerville School District is a composite of several schools we've worked with, we are using authentic examples and experiences to show how you can implement respect, impulse control, compassion, and equity in your school. We organized each chapter of this book to illustrate how a typical school district can use the content of the curriculum; the structure of the school day; the sequence of the school year; and the counseling, discipline, and safety practices to provide all members of the school community with meaningful opportunities to use RICE (respect, impulse control, compassion, and equity). From the hallway to the classroom, the athletic program to the parent-teacher conference, and through each step of professional development, we illustrate how a school district can use the character and conduct approach to help students learn and stay safe.

1

Getting Started

Once again, Pat, a 6th grade teacher at Centerville Middle School, is surprised at how hard it is to fall asleep the night before the first day of school. She tells herself that it doesn't matter whether it's a teacher's first year of teaching or twenty-first, the night before school begins is filled with excitement, nervousness, hope, and a sense of the unknown. Each year, Pat asks the same questions: What will my students be like? How will I get them through the new assessments? Will I have a support team? What will the principal want? Will the parents be supportive? As she waits for the sun to rise, thoughts about the new standards, increased accountability, and new technology race through her head. "Am I ready for all this?" she wonders.

Pat's sleepless scenario is played by many educators the night before every opening day. As teachers, administrators, pupil personnel, and support staff, we have countless "getting started" questions about the growing pressures and responsibilities that schools face. Traditionally, we have heard conflicting answers to our questions, and we have prepared for our work in isolation. As a result, each year we feel increasingly overwhelmed by how much we have to teach, test, and report. Uninterrupted instructional time is rare, and the responsibility for achieving safe schools competes with the need to help all students meet new rigorous academic standards.

Although Pat, like many of her colleagues, is nervous and sleepless the day before school opens, she approaches the coming school year with confidence. She knows that her school's principal, teachers, pupil personnel (e.g., guidance counselors, psychologists, social workers, nurses), and support staff have agreed that with all the demands on their limited time, they need to depend on one another to create and support shared goals. This year, the administration, faculty, and staff will promote the same standards for learning, character, and conduct. As a result, Pat and her colleagues have some answers in common to their questions:

- School has a core purpose: to help all children learn and apply what they learn within and beyond school.
- The members of the school community include educators, parents, and students.
- Each member has a role in ensuring that the school achieves its purpose for all students.
- All members follow the same guiding principles—respect, impulse control, compassion, and equity—to promote the purpose of school.

Pat's confidence is also bolstered by the implementation plan that she and her colleagues have crafted to establish how they will achieve goals by using the existing curriculum, discipline, and counseling programs. This shared foundation is important to school life for two reasons: (1) it establishes a strong majority commitment to shared goals, principles, and practices; and (2) it aligns the teaching, discipline, and counseling components of school activity so that everyone works toward the same goals.

Pat prepared for the first day by following a standards-driven plan that included

- Measurable goals for student learning and conduct
- Strategies and materials to achieve those goals
- Strategies and materials to measure and report progress.

Every member of the school community has a plan to start the year. Teams of administrators, teachers, and pupil personnel developed their plans through a process that can be explained in this book and duplicated by schools and school districts. The process begins with an awareness of a problem and a desire for change.

Several years ago, Pat and many of her colleagues had observed that students were disrespectful to one another and to adults. Their attitude undermined the teaching and learning process. Administrators were inundated with disciplinary referrals, which resulted in fewer hours to dedicate to the instructional leadership that affects students' academic performance. Parents expressed their concerns about the safety and the climate of the school, as well as about test score results and new state requirements. Counselors, psychologists, and other pupil personnel raised similar concerns at their meetings. Even students complained about bullies, harassment, and incidents of disrespect by fellow students and some staff members. Everyone had the same question: What can we do to make things better?

To answer this question, a team from the Centerville Middle School staff researched ways to enhance student learning, improve school climate, and promote school safety. They chose to use four guiding principles: respect, impulse control, compassion, and equity (RICE) to create an approach that would improve school life. The program was not envisioned as an add-on program—it was to become a part of school life. Integrating guiding principles into the existing school curriculum, discipline program, and counseling program offered the best use of time. After the team presented the idea at a faculty meeting, the majority of the staff agreed to participate actively.

Assessing Needs

During the summer, the Centerville Middle School administrators, faculty, and support staff participated in a two-day professional development workshop[1] that helped them design their instructional plans for the upcoming school year. They did a careful needs assessment to determine the school's problems and strengths (see Appendix A). Next, they decided where they wanted to be at the end of the school year. Finally, they inventoried the resources they could use to achieve their goals and named the obstacles that could undermine their progress. Figure 1.1 shows some of what the staff learned.

The Centerville Middle School team used the results of the needs assessment to determine what each member of the school could do to close the gap between where they were and where they wanted to be. They agreed to adhere to the guiding principles of respect, impulse control, compassion, and equity (RICE) and to teach these principles through four major areas of school activity: all curricular areas; the schoolwide discipline program; the advisory program facilitated by the pupil personnel team; and a program that focuses on communication between home and school. The team created charts demonstrating how each guiding principle would be modeled in classrooms and in other areas of the school (see Figure 1.2).

Identifying Roles

After they completed the needs assessment and reached their basic agreements, the Centerville Middle School team began to work in groups of up to 10 members, organized according to each person's role in the building: one group of administrators, four groups of teachers, and one group of pupil personnel and staff members. Each group's task was to determine how its members could work within

---

[1] The workshop, the Circle of Character and Conduct, is a complement to this book. Contact the authors for more information.

Figure 1.1—Assessing Our Needs

Listing the concerns that staff and community express about your school can be useful in addressing the problem. In addition, consider how you can monitor progress toward your goal—such as by tracking a decrease in disciplinary referrals.

What student behaviors are causing concern?	• Calling out • Interrupting one another • Speaking disrespectfully and impulsively • Not listening to or following directions
What evidence do we have of these behaviors?	• Incident reports, discipline referrals, suspensions, and detentions • Letters to parents and guardians about disciplinary issues • Fights and bus incidents
How do we want students to behave?	• Listen to the end of other people's sentences • Control impulses to speak out of turn • Listen for understanding • Speak respectfully • Follow directions
What resources do we have to help students close the gap between what we observe and our goals?	• Teaching and counseling skills (modeling and direct instruction) • English language arts across the curriculum • Discipline program
What obstacles may prevent us from reaching our goals?	• Inconsistent application of behavior expectations • Lack of support from other stakeholders in the building • Miscommunication among stakeholders
How will we monitor progress?	• Set benchmarks • Schedule assessments of implementation and student learning • Modify implementation as needed

Figure 1.2—Examples of RICE

RICE is the acronym for the guiding principles of respect, impulse control, compassion, and equity.

Respect	Impulse control	Compassion	Equity
Looks like	*Looks like*	*Looks like*	*Looks like*
• Listening • Walking appropriately through the halls	• Waiting turns • Modeling and observing classroom rules and procedures	• Offering help • Accepting help	• Seeing that everyone gets whatever is necessary for success • Having everyone participate and be accepted
Sounds like	*Sounds like*	*Sounds like*	*Sounds like*
• "What do you think?" • "Help me understand . . ."	• Using an appropriate tone, even when we feel impatient or angry • "We need some time to consider the best choice in this circumstance."	• "Would you like some help?" • "We can do this together."	• "Everyone is a member of our team." • "Everyone has an important role in helping our group succeed."

their specific roles to help all students learn and follow the guiding principles of RICE. The groups brainstormed about how they could incorporate the guiding principles into everyday lessons, disciplinary procedures, and counseling activities. They all considered how they could apply the new approach to central categories of school activity:

• Schoolwide activities, such as assemblies and pep rallies, to establish a school climate promoting learning, character, and conduct

• Prevention activities to help establish baseline standards for student conduct

• Disciplinary activities to correct behaviors that interfere with the purpose of Centerville Middle School

• Monitoring and evaluation efforts to gauge the effectiveness of the new schoolwide activities throughout the school year

For example, the four teams of teachers decided to organize their classroom management routines to help students follow rules and procedures for listening, contributing, and following directions. In the interest of promoting school safety and preventing violence, the counselors determined that they would encourage students to reach out for help in appropriate ways by using respect, impulse control, compassion, and equity. They would focus on supporting students when they ask for help, listen to instructions, follow anger-management plans, and complete academic work in a timely fashion. The administrative team responded to the principal's concerns about working with the 5 percent of students who take up 95 percent of the administrative disciplinary time. Specifically, the administrators decided to use a behavior replacement action plan that includes specific roles for the student, teachers, administrators, pupil personnel, parents, and others involved with the student.

The teams used the information in Figure 1.3 to add, remove, or improve their teaching, discipline, and counseling activities. The goal was to have a positive effect on student learning, character, and conduct. For example, Joseph Santo, a veteran physical education teacher, observed that the same students usually repeated disruptive behaviors despite the system of rewards, punishments, and reports to teachers and parents. On the basis of the planning table, Mr. Santo and his team members developed an instructional plan that used the existing unit on teamwork in the physical education curriculum. Now their unit focuses on teaching students how to replace disrup-

---

Figure 1.3—Assessing Teaching and Activities

Use the following criteria to assess your teaching, discipline, and counseling activities for effectiveness.

A program is most likely to directly affect student learning and conduct if it is
- Standards-driven
- Integrated into the existing curriculum
- Designed with developmentally appropriate strategies and activities
- Driven by the guiding principles of respect, impulse control, compassion, and equity
- Research-based
- Based on district or building goals
- Congruent with existing discipline policies and programs
- Congruent with existing counseling programs
- Aligned with standards for communication between home and school
- Supported schoolwide by administrators, teachers, and pupil personnel
- Supported in practice among teachers, administrators, and pupil personnel
- Designed to give direct instruction of expected outcomes

A program is not likely to affect student learning and conduct if it is
- A stand-alone program
- Not based on needs assessment
- Not supported schoolwide
- Not uniformly supported by stakeholders with common goals
- Not communicated to the parents and school community

---

tive behavior with alternatives based on RICE. They used the table to ensure that their teaching strategies and materials met the criteria for positively affecting student learning and conduct. For example, in a final activity on teamwork, students practice being the coach. In assuming that role, the students analyze videotapes, just as the coach would, to identify strengths and weaknesses and to help individuals work on strategies to improve the team as a whole.

In the language arts area, Pat expressed her frustration with students who call out continually, interrupting her and other students in the middle of a lesson. The 6th grade teachers agreed to address the interruptions through the English language arts curriculum.

They decided to teach the students to demonstrate respect by listen-ing carefully and waiting their turn to speak. The teachers would measure student learning by observing students to see if they began to listen to the end of another person's sentence and were control-ling the impulse to speak while another person was talking. The teachers agreed that they would model the listening and speaking behaviors they expected from their students.

The administrative team, led by Principal Rutledge, agreed to model and support the listening and speaking behaviors being taught by the 6th grade team. For example, Mr. Hawkins, a social studies teacher, referred Laurie to Mrs. Carter, the assistant princi-pal, for continually calling out in class and repeatedly refusing to take direction.

Mrs. Carter took Laurie through three steps. First, she required Laurie to complete one day of in-school suspension. Second, during the suspension, Mrs. Carter and Laurie created a behavior replace-ment plan to help Laurie apply respect and impulse control as she listens, contributes, and follows directions in class. Mrs. Carter referred to what Laurie is learning about citizenship and laws in her social studies class and engaged her in practicing the guiding princi-ples and techniques in their conversation. Third, Mrs. Carter and Laurie made an appointment for Laurie to meet with the guidance counselor, Mr. Bryant, who can monitor and support her progress.

The members of the pupil personnel team constructed their own plans to help students use the guiding principles in all their commu-nications and decision making, with special attention directed at lis-tening and speaking for social interaction and understanding. For instance, Laurie and Mr. Bryant made a series of six appointments to help her practice listening skills and to assess her progress as reported by the teachers and administrators. Laurie and Mr. Bryant called her parents to report the results of their meeting; he contin-ues to involve them in her progress. Laurie's parents were pleased with her progress, after expressing some initial concern and surprise at the call. They were aware of the school's new approach to student learning and conduct, having received information from the Centerville Middle School's parent newsletter. The newsletter contained tips for parents and guardians based on the four guiding principles of respect, impulse control, compassion, and equity.

All the teams developed parent tips that were published in the school's newsletter, suggesting how parents can help students by using the guiding principles at home and in the community. For example, the school recommended that parents create a regular time in their day or evening to listen to their child read aloud the teacher's directions for homework and other schoolwork. In this way, the student reviews the teacher's expectations and the parents learn what the student is doing in school. The school also suggested that parent and child agree to listen to the end of each other's sentences and to check for understanding. A simple practice sheet is sent home to help families develop this skill.

These are just a few representative examples from a school plan for aligning teaching, discipline, and counseling practices to support student learning, character, and conduct. The expectation is that disciplinary problems will decrease, time on task will increase, and school climate will improve. The plan includes monitoring the indicators identified in the needs assessment (see Appendix A). The monitoring process matches the existing school routines for collecting data:

• Monthly counts of attendance, discipline referrals, and incidents of violence and weapons possession
• Interim reports, report cards, and test results
• Ongoing personal feedback from teachers, administrators, and pupil personnel, as well as from students and parents

The staff, students, and parents agreed to use these data to evaluate, continue, and correct their activities. For instance, Cecile Lund, a 7th grade math teacher, asked her department members to conduct a quarterly assessment to determine how teaching listening skills affects student conduct and math achievement. Prior to adopting the guiding principles, the math department had been concerned that teaching students listening skills would take instructional time away from helping students master the knowledge and skills required by the national and state standards and assessments. When they compare this year's attendance, discipline, and math test data with next year's data, the department members have agreed to evaluate the answers to the following questions:

• Are the students following directions more quickly and correctly?

• Has lateness decreased? Has general attendance improved?

• Are teachers spending less time correcting student behavior and repeating directions?

• Are teachers spending more time actively engaging students in math activities?

• Are students completing homework more consistently and correctly?

• Are students generally more successful on teacher-generated tests?

• Have students achieved at or above previous years' scores on standardized tests?

Cecile Lund and her math team plan to evaluate the new approach in math by answering these questions on a quarterly basis throughout the school year. They will take the next step to create their plan by following the guidelines for the first 10 days of school (see Chapter 2).

Figure 1.4—Demonstrations of Appropriate Respect and Listening Behaviors

Elementary school

Goal: To improve student respect, listening, and speaking during whole-group instruction.

Mrs. Glenn, a 1st grade teacher, teaches her students to raise their hands to ask questions or share thoughts. She helps the students understand that she may call on them to share their thoughts even if their hands are not raised.

When Mrs. Glenn calls on one student, the other students follow a simple procedure:

- Lower all hands.
- Listen to the end of the other person's sentence.
- Look at the person who is speaking.
- Be prepared to comment on special points that the person might have made.
- Listen for the teacher's directions.

For example, when Mrs. Glenn calls on Molly, all other students put their hands down and listen until Molly has finished her response.

High school

Goal: To improve student respect, listening, and speaking during cooperative-learning activities.

In his 11th grade chemistry lab, Mr. Elmore assigns students to work in heterogeneously grouped teams to complete laboratory activities. Students must listen to and follow directions so that everyone stays safe and successfully completes the lab experiment. Everyone has a different role in the lab activity, but each role involves listening and speaking at appropriate times.

Mr. Elmore begins each lab by demonstrating the steps the students will follow and requiring the students to check for their own understanding before they begin the experiment. As a matter of routine, Mr. Elmore expects the students to

- Listen to directions as he states them
- Restate the directions in their own words so that they can check for their own understanding and that of their lab partners
- Apply the same listening and checking for understanding skills in their cooperative lab groups

In this chapter, we focused on Centerville Middle School staff and students. In subsequent chapters, we will illustrate each phase of implementation through the activities of the Centerville elementary, middle, and high schools. Although each chapter illustrates the experiences of one school in particular, we will provide some examples of how schools at other levels can use similar steps to achieve their goals. Figure 1.4 outlines an example of how the guiding principles approach may be used in elementary schools and high schools.

2

The First Ten Days

"This year will be different," asserts Joe DeLuca, a 4th grade teacher at Centerville Elementary School, as he walks into the faculty room.

"You say the same thing every year, Joe! Sit down and have a cup of coffee," laughed Marion Brown, who's been teaching 3rd grade across the hall from Joe for the past seven years.

"I really mean it this time," Joe counters. "This year, we're setting the rules right from the start. Assignments will be in on time. They'll really listen, they'll really learn. I'm starting them off the right way this year."

Conversations like this one are typical before the start of school. Teachers feel refreshed and renewed after a summer break. Educators return to school filled with high expectations and resolutions that this year will be better. Too often, the high expectations dissipate as teachers experience the competing pressures of state assessments, curriculum mandates, disciplinary issues, individual student needs, and parental concerns. Students also experience the competing pressures of academic responsibilities, out-of-school activities, and family priorities. Pressures on both teachers and students weaken academic focus; behavior problems are an added distraction.

In the past, Centerville Elementary School staff addressed these issues through one-day, add-on character education and disciplinary programs, such as poster contests, word-of-the-day activities, short-run service learning activities, fund-raising functions, special assembly programs, incentive programs, and theme-of-the-month initiatives. Although the programs set important goals for student behavior, staff agreed that the students did not connect the programs and everyday school life in a way that could sustain the desired behaviors. In fact, the staff believed that the effects of these programs were short term and that the process interrupted the instructional program. They were also concerned that these programs did not address the "hidden curriculum"—the contradiction between the formal lessons taught in class and actions of educators and other adults and students in and out of the classroom.

During a summer workshop that introduced the connecting character and conduct program, Centerville staff heard a story about a fire drill that serves as an example of the contradictory messages in the hidden curriculum. The story begins with a teacher conducting emergency exit lessons that focus on how staying silent during an exit drill can keep everyone safe. During an actual drill, however, the teacher talks with colleagues while leaving the building. When the students see the difference between the formal lessons and the teacher's actions, the hidden curriculum undermines classroom instruction.

This year, staff members have developed plans to close the gap between what they teach in formal lessons and what they practice throughout the school. As a result, the educators have replaced the hidden curriculum with opportunities for students and staff to apply the guiding principles of respect, impulse control, compassion, and equity in formal and informal interactions throughout the school day.

The guiding principles help sustain the high expectations and academic focus at Centerville Elementary School, despite competing pressures. The administrators, teachers, pupil personnel, and other staff are following the plans they developed during the Character and Conduct workshop to align their teaching, disciplinary, and counseling practices. Together, they created a schoolwide plan that includes individual plans for classroom teachers, administrators, pupil personnel, and other school staff to follow in the first 10 days of school. These plans are basic to replacing the hidden curriculum for all members of the Centerville Elementary School community.

On the basis of the needs assessment completed during the summer workshop, the Centerville Elementary School staff worked in teams to select strategies, activities, and materials from the available options. The teams were organized so that the teachers met in groups of five members, the four building-level administrators met as one team, and the eight pupil personnel staff worked together. In their separate teams, they selected specific approaches to help all the students learn school and classroom rules, procedures, goals, and roles during the first 10 days of the school year.

Teacher Planning

Joe DeLuca agreed with his colleagues that the results of the needs assessment were on target: Students needed to improve the way they treated one another in the classroom and throughout the school. Mrs. Brown had told Mr. DeLuca that his incoming 4th grade class included a mix of students with challenging behaviors. Some showed positive leadership qualities, others had been victimized, and still others had bullied their classmates. Mr. DeLuca understood that his classroom management plan must match this blend of student strengths and needs.

Mr. DeLuca began the year by teaching his students what respect should look, sound, and feel like in their class as they follow their daily routines and activities. He helped his students develop a plan to apply the principles of respect, impulse control, compassion, and equity in all their classroom and school activities. His students collaboratively wrote the first element of the class constitution: All members of the school community are entitled to respect. The class constructed a list of ideas that illustrate what respect looks, sounds, and feels like. Using that list, the students developed an agreement and followed a plan to demonstrate respectful behaviors in the classroom, in the hallway, in the midday assembly program, and during transitions, including lunch, recess, and dismissal (see Figure 2.1).

Mr. DeLuca's students wrote a letter to their parents and guardians to explain the goal of Centerville Elementary School; the goal of their class; their roles as learners within that class; their teachers' role; the parent's or guardian's role in supporting the student's learning; guiding principles (RICE); and procedures for succeeding in class. A sample letter appears as Figure 2.2. They directed

---

Figure 2.1—Student Agreement for Respect

We demonstrate respect by
• Listening to the end of other people's sentences
• Walking quietly and attentively through the halls
• Raising our hands to participate in whole-group instruction

We demonstrate respect when we use certain statements, such as
• What do you think?
• Let's agree to disagree.
• We'll try this together.

I, _____ , agree to practice these behaviors to achieve the best learning environment for everyone at my school.

Our guiding principle is respect, because respect can make us feel
• Good about our learning
• Confident that we can succeed, even when we need help
• Important, as members of our class and school

_____

(signature)

Figure 2.2—4th Graders Explain RICE

Dear Mom and Dad,

This letter is to tell you about some new things happening in my class and my school. My teacher, Mr. DeLuca, explained that our class is a team. We have a goal, and we each have a special role on our team.

Our goal is to learn and to be safe. Our role is to do and say things that help everybody learn and be safe. Mr. DeLuca's special role is to be like our coach. All the students have to be prepared for school, do homework, and do a good job in class. That's how we become a good team.

Our class made rules to achieve our goals. Our rules are about using Respect, Impulse Control, Compassion, Equity. That spells RICE! Our whole school agreed to follow the same rules!

You have a special role, too. Help me practice following RICE at home, and help me get ready for school every day.

---

special attention to being prepared, completing homework, and participating appropriately in class.

Mr. DeLuca organized activities to involve his students in integrated lessons that could help them demonstrate the appropriate learning and conduct measured in all instructional settings and in the discipline and counseling programs within the school. Figure 2.3 shows how teaching, learning, disciplinary practices, counsel, and support activities can be integrated to help students demonstrate respect.

Using Figure 2.3 as a visual organizer, Mr. DeLuca decided how to integrate his instructional, support, and discipline activities within the classroom. The principal, Mrs. Griffin, and the other members of the administrative and pupil personnel teams used the same visual organizer to create their integrated plans.

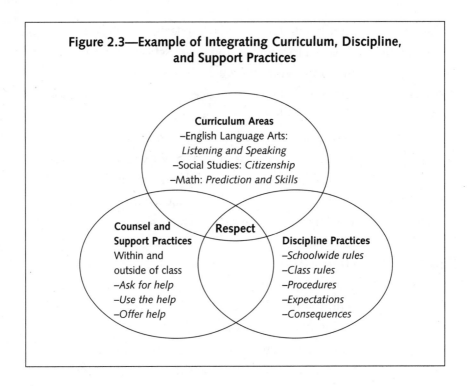

Figure 2.3—Example of Integrating Curriculum, Discipline, and Support Practices

Curriculum Areas
–English Language Arts: *Listening and Speaking*
–Social Studies: *Citizenship*
–Math: *Prediction and Skills*

Counsel and Support Practices
Within and outside of class
–Ask for help
–Use the help
–Offer help

Respect

Discipline Practices
–Schoolwide rules
–Class rules
–Procedures
–Expectations
–Consequences

Administrator Planning

Mrs. Griffin worked with the team of administrators to integrate the guiding principles of respect, impulse control, compassion, and equity into their instructional leadership practices and disciplinary activities. Because the summer workshop included opportunities for each team to share plans and priorities, the administrators knew that the teachers were using the English language arts, social studies, and math curricula to teach students about RICE during the first 10 days.

Mrs. Griffin's priorities for the same 10 days were (1) to lead and support the instructional program the teachers developed in the Circle of Character and Conduct summer workshops, and (2) to ensure that Centerville Elementary School's discipline practices realistically guide students to apply the skills and knowledge they learn in the classroom. The entire administrative team agreed that these priorities are directly related to maintaining a safe school environment and to continually improving student learning. To help staff and students apply the principles and practices of RICE in the school, Mrs. Griffin began the Welcome Back assembly with a slide show illustrating that the purpose of Centerville Elementary School is to help children learn in a safe environment. She explained that each member of the school has a role in fulfilling that purpose and that everyone can use the guiding principles to succeed. The teachers know that she expects them to reinforce and assess student learning about the school's purpose as well as the roles and rules learned in the assembly and to reteach that information as needed. In addition, the principal monitors students during arrival and dismissal, in the lunchroom, and during recess activities and uses the guiding principles to help the students apply the RICE skills taught in the classroom. To check on the students' progress, teachers, administrators, and others share observations about how the students are applying RICE schoolwide.

Mrs. Griffin also applied her "first 10 days" plan in disciplinary activities. She met individually with two students referred to her for fighting in the cafeteria. In these meetings, they discussed the context of the conflict, what went wrong, the alternatives available to the student, and the consequences that follow the student's behavior. As a culminating step, Mrs. Griffin had each student complete a template to create a behavior replacement plan. Here is an example of a completed form:

1. What rules did I break? *I broke the rules that require respect and impulse control.*
2. What role did I not fulfill? *I did not fulfill my role as a learner and a person who must help keep our school safe.*
3. What will I do and say the next time I feel like repeating this behavior? *The next time I feel like fighting I will concentrate on how I want to be free to eat lunch with my friends and stay in class instead*

of going to in-school suspension. I will use RICE to help me. I know it will be hard. One way I can use RICE is to walk away instead of fighting.

4. What will happen as a result of my behavior? *I will be suspended in-school for one day and I will not be able to eat lunch in the cafeteria for a week.*

5. What will happen when I follow the rules? *I will be able to attend class with my friends and eat lunch with my friends in the cafeteria.*

The students presented their behavior replacement plans to their teachers and worked with their administrator, teachers, and counselor to make modifications. Mrs. Griffin enforced the school disciplinary policy on fighting and coordinated communication among home, teachers, pupil personnel, and students. She also put into place a plan to monitor, assess, and adjust the students' behavior replacement plans.

Pupil Personnel Planning

The "first 10 days" plan developed by Steve Mohr, the school's social worker, and the other members of Centerville Elementary School's pupil personnel team, helps students make connections with members of the pupil personnel team. These connections are especially important during the transitional days of school, because the social worker, school nurse, and other members of the team are uniquely equipped to reduce student alienation and to manage the discomfort with which many students struggle daily.

Mr. Mohr participated in creating and narrating the Welcome Back assembly slide show illustrating the purpose of Centerville Elementary School. He explained how he and the other members of the pupil personnel team are there to help the students and to promote the guiding principles throughout the school. Mr. Mohr and Olympia Vitalis, the school's nurse, greet students during arrival and touch base during dismissal, in the lunchroom, and during recess. They work together to support student use of the guiding principles. Through informal contacts and formal conference settings, pupil personnel staff members reinforce student learning regarding the purpose of the school and related rules and roles.

The social worker and the school nurse also had roles in dealing with the cafeteria fight between the two students. Mrs. Griffin contacted Mrs. Vitalis to tend to minor cuts and Mr. Mohr to follow up on the students' behavior replacement plans. In conjunction with the classroom teacher, Mr. Mohr made the appropriate contacts with home and provided the counsel and support necessary to help the students involved follow their behavior replacement plan. All of the adults reinforced RICE skills.

Planning for Parent Support

In the back-to-school edition of the principal's newsletter to the parents and guardians of the Centerville Elementary School students, Mrs. Griffin introduced the guiding principles. Every team contributed tips suggesting how parents can help their children succeed during the first 10 days of school. For example, the teams suggested that parents help children decide when and where homework will be completed each day. They also recommended that parents have their children explain what RICE means in Centerville Elementary School.

Joe DeLuca, Marion Brown, Meredith Griffin, Steve Mohr, and their colleagues at Centerville Elementary School designed their "first 10 days" plans to help students learn the purpose, roles, rules, and procedures and meet members of their school and classes. They used the guiding principles to strengthen their individual and collective efforts to help each student achieve intended goals within the 10-day framework. In this fashion, they established the normative

---

Figure 2.4—Strategies for Secondary Students

The following strategies are useful in teaching students to attend class on time, to be prepared, and to follow classroom procedures. These strategies can be used anytime or throughout the school year, but are especially effective in setting expectations for the first 10 days of school.

- Mr. Ling, a 6th grade teacher, uses a visual "do now" approach in the first few minutes of each class to reinforce homework and ensure punctuality. He writes an assignment on the board or shows a video clip to immediately involve students during the first three to five minutes of class. The assignment is related to the homework and the class work and is evaluated by the teacher.

- Ms. Jack helps the students in her science classes understand the connection between the guiding principles and her classroom procedures through a contract-writing activity centering on safety in the lab.

- Mr. Barber's art class illustrates what respect looks and sounds like in the art room, with special attention directed at distributing materials, cleaning up, and tolerating different levels of talent and different ideas.

- In Mr. Weber's 10th grade social studies class, students make journal entries within the first five minutes of class as they reflect on a key idea from the previous assignment and anticipate the connection to today's new learning.

- Senora Ramos immerses her second-year Spanish students in a listening exercise for the first two minutes of each class. In the first 10 days, the students listen for the Spanish words for respect, impulse control, compassion, and equity: *respeto, dominio de sí mismo, compasión, equidad.*

- Mr. Leonard's technology class follows a classroom safety procedure based on RICE with special emphasis on using impulse control around equipment.

---

structure for the remainder of the school year. Figure 2.4 illustrates how middle and high school educators used their 10-day plans.

With the first 10 days successfully completed, Centerville Elementary School staff, along with their colleagues on the secondary levels, directed their attention to the rest school year. In Chapter 3, we chart an average school day and school year through the experiences of the Centerville High School students and staff.

3

Finding the Time

Erica took a deep breath as she walked into Centerville High School for her first full day of class as a sophomore. She still couldn't believe that her parents had moved to a totally different community right in the middle of her high school life. All her friends were miles away. She would never really see them the way she used to. With whom would she have lunch every day? She didn't even remember where her locker was. That whole orientation thing sounded good but slightly confusing. What was all that stuff about everyone in the school following the same guiding principles? She felt as if everyone were looking at her. Things here seemed different. She didn't know exactly why. "Whatever," she thought. "I'd better get to first period on time. They made a big deal about that at orientation. Here goes."

What Erica is about to find out is that all the "stuff" she heard about at orientation is really the way all the members of the Centerville High School community interact daily. Centerville High School has integrated the guiding principles of respect, impulse control, compassion, and equity into school life. Changes have already occurred in the way all members of the school community approach day-to-day interactions, including teaching, learning, counseling, and discipline. Students understand that the purpose of school is to help everyone learn and stay safe. Students know that they have a role in fulfilling that purpose and understand that the school calendar is organized to help them.

For example, the teachers expect all students to use the student handbook that summarizes the guiding principles and their applications (see samples pages from the student handbook in Appendix B). This year, the *Centerville High School Chronicle* featured a special section for parents before the school year started. It described the homework and attendance policies in the student handbook, as well as the role of parents as partners in the education of high school students (see Figure 3.1).

In Erica's previous school, no one specifically taught students that there is a shared purpose to schooling. No one clarified the special role that students have in helping themselves and others

---

Figure 3.1—Centerville Homework Guide

The student handbook includes many tips for students, from the guiding principles to the homework guide. The following excerpt is from the homework section.

1. Put assignments in order of priority for dates due.
2. Estimate how much time each will take and what materials you will need. Begin doing the assignments in order of due dates.
3. Read the teacher's directions completely.
   a. If you understand the directions, consider how the work relates to today's lesson and how the teacher could use the homework in tomorrow's lesson.
   b. If you don't understand the directions, check in with another student or friend. If no one is available, write a note to the teacher explaining your confusion. Be specific.
4. Complete homework tasks in order.
5. When mom or dad comes home, share one way the homework related to class work and one way it might be used in class the next day. If mom or dad isn't home yet, have this discussion with a classmate or a friend.
6. Put all homework together and make it ready to take to school the next school day.

learn, and no one demonstrated how students could use the school calendar to achieve academic goals. In her other school, there wasn't a student handbook, and rules and discipline procedures varied from class to class and from administrator to administrator. Erica's new high school was definitely different.

The First Month of School

Ms. Barett, the assistant principal of Centerville High School, noticed that Erica looked confused and helped her find her first-period social studies class. As a member of the administrative team, she was pleased to see that the halls were clear at the sound of the bell, even on the first day of school. All the administrators were in the halls, making sure that students moved quickly and safely to their scheduled destinations. Ms. Barett attributed this accomplishment to the planning that she and the other administrators had completed during the summer Circle of Character and Conduct workshop. Their action plan to support school safety by using the daily schedule has several components:

• "Managing by wandering around" to monitor classrooms, halls, and school grounds
• Enforcing on-grounds parking permit requirements
• Communicating with parents about what they can do to help their children arrive on time to each class, ready to learn
• Using the computer attendance system to monitor student attendance, period by period
• Involving the guidance counselors, deans, truant officers, attendance teachers, and other support staff (including such non-school employees as youth counselors, probation officers, drug counselors, police officers, and security personnel) in reaching out to students with a history of attendance-related problems

Consistent with the administrative plan, Ms. Barett walked Erica into her social studies class. Erica noticed that all the students were already engaged in an activity at their desks. The teacher, Mr. Weber, smiled and welcomed her to the class; he seated her with a team of students who were expecting her. Jeff, the team facilitator for the task, greeted Erica and handed her a worksheet for their first day of school. He explained that students often work in teams at Centerville High and that they had five minutes to complete a brainstorming activity for the first day of school.

Erica breathed a sigh of relief as she completed the activity. In her other school, many of her classes did not really get going until the teacher had finished taking attendance and dealing with other clerical tasks. In this class, the teacher seemed to get all that done while the students were engaged in a content-based assignment.

Dawn, another member of her team, told Erica that all the classes start like this and that all students are expected to get to class on time. This emphasis on punctuality comes from a yearlong effort on the part of Centerville High School staff to teach the students the school rules and expectations and to measure the results of that instruction. The administrators, the teachers, and other staff used the needs assessment and input from the community to organize their instructional, counseling, and discipline activities around the daily school schedule and the academic year.

The importance of getting to school and to class on time and of keeping the hallways safe and orderly, as well as the value of prompt staff outreach to students, emerged from the needs assessment the staff completed. These outcomes were consistent with feedback from parents, school board members, and other community leaders who, over the past several years, had expressed concerns about alienated students, cliques, students who cut class, and students who wandered around the building and the community during school hours.

By addressing these concerns, the Centerville High School staff expect to reach their goals for increased instructional time and safe schools. Staff members developed and followed their "first 10 days" plans to teach students how to use the daily schedule to their advantage. Mr. Weber used his plan to teach students how to develop their own methods for getting to class on time and completing assignments. His strategy involves an assignment that he calls a "do now," which is to be done in the first five minutes of class. The assignment is often a journal entry in which the students reflect on a key idea from the previous assignment and anticipate the connection to new learning. Mr. Weber also introduced the 10th grade social studies students to the important concept of governance. In one instance, the "do now" was a document by Aristotle about the need for and purpose of government. With this assignment, Mr. Weber helped the students transfer centuries-old governance theory to everyday life at Centerville High School. On the first day of class and throughout the first month, the transfer of learning focused on the purpose of school and the role of the individual within a larger social system. Mr. Weber required his students to

- Create a plan they would follow to learn the daily school schedule
  - Integrate the schedule into their daily routines
  - Organize time to complete their homework
  - Arrive at class ready to learn and participate

Mr. Weber moved the students through the lesson by helping them construct the graphic organizer in Figure 3.2, which demonstrates the connection between the concept of governance and everyday student life. This is just one example of how Mr. Weber introduced his class rules and procedures during the first month of school. The other staff members at Centerville High School fol-

Figure 3.2—Governance and Everyday Student Life

As a "do now" exercise, Mr. Weber's class compared governance in ancient Greece with Centerville High School's governing principles.

Government in Ancient Greece
Purpose: Foster a democratic society ruled by the people to
• Ensure safety
• Educate citizens
• Protect rights
• Establish the role of the citizen as a member of society

Citizen-Student

Centerville High School
Purpose: Foster a school community dedicated to learning and character to
• Ensure safety
• Promote learning
• Protect rights
• Establish the role of the student as a contributing member of the school and community

The citizen upholds the purpose by
• Following laws
• Participating in government
• Promoting personal and general welfare

The citizen-student's long-term goal is to graduate and continue to be a contributing member of society by
• Following rules (RICE) and procedures
• Participating in learning
• Promoting personal and general welfare

Specifically, the citizen upholds society by
• Being a productive member of society
• Paying taxes
• Voting
• Considering the rights and needs of oneself and other citizens

Specifically, the citizen-student upholds society and learning by
• Attending class
• Being punctual
• Completing homework
• Being prepared
• Thinking critically and applying skills and knowledge to everyday life

lowed similar plans that linked the roles of the students with central areas of curriculum, instruction, and discipline. Common themes for the first month related to fostering increased instructional time and achieving a safe school by improving class attendance and punctuality, improving the rate of homework completions, and involving students in classroom and school activities.

These lessons served as a review for Jeff and for the other students at Centerville who were familiar with the guiding principles. It was a novel learning experience for Erica and the other new members of the Centerville High School community, whose former schools failed to make such a clear connection among learning, school safety, and personal responsibility.

Along with the other teachers in the high school, Mr. Weber expects the students to use their handbook as part of their daily routine. He organizes his lessons to help students connect their graduation goals to their daily decisions and activities. Mr. Weber's lessons for the first 10 days were designed to help students discover that they can use the principles of respect, impulse control, compassion, and equity to remain focused on their goals and to support one another's learning. All students create a profile of an average school day to help them visualize how to fulfill their responsibilities as students and as citizens of the high school community. Mr. Weber encouraged them to consider other time pressures, such as family responsibilities, work, and extracurricular activities, as well as their own procrastination, to meet their obligations.

Erica's outline of her school day is shown in Figure 3.3. Using the plan was a struggle for her during the first month of school. When she was scheduled to do homework, she wanted to talk with her friends from her former high school. This was a real conflict for her, but Erica concentrated on practicing impulse control in three major areas of her school life: (1) completing her homework as scheduled; (2) getting to school and class on time; and (3) calling a

Time	Activity	✔
Figure 3.3—Erica's Daily School Plan		
5:50–6:50 a.m.	Up on time. Shower, do hair, get dressed, grab breakfast, check in with family calendar for the day (do I have to pick up my little sister, get the dry cleaning?). Set VCR for daytime TV shows.	
6:50–6:55 a.m.	Check to make sure I have everything I need for school in my backpack: homework? keys? money for lunch? Check on the dog and lock the door.	
6:55–7:00 a.m.	Walk to bus stop. Hope it's on time!	
7:00–7:20 a.m.	Ride the bus. Make sure I take everything with me when I get off.	
7:20–7:30 a.m.	Get to locker, check hair, get the right books and stuff for morning classes. Make sure I have the homework I did last night.	
7:30–7:40 a.m.	Get to first-period class on time and begin "do now."	
7:30 a.m.–2:20 p.m.	Use class and school schedule to organize the day until the last class is over at 2:20 p.m.	
2:20–2:30 p.m.	Back to locker to get stuff for PSAT prep class. Go to PSAT prep.	
2:30–3:00 p.m.	Attend PSAT prep class.	
3:00–3:10 p.m.	Get to locker, drop off PSAT stuff, pick up homework material, and board late bus home.	
3:10–3:30 p.m.	Ride late bus home. Take everything with me when I leave the bus.	
3:30–4:30 p.m.	Bring in the mail. Drop off backpack and school stuff in kitchen. Take care of the dog. Check messages. Call Mom and tell her I'm home. Talk with friends on the phone. Wait for Carrie to get home from school.	
4:30–5:30 p.m.	Watch tapes of TV shows I recorded. Baby-sit Carrie.	
5:30–6:00 p.m.	Help Carrie empty dishwasher, set table, do other dinner prep stuff.	
6:00–6:30 p.m.	Have dinner, clean up. Review all assignments due for this week.	
6:30–8:00 p.m.	Start homework. Follow the homework guide to do my homework. Put my homework in my backpack and put the backpack by the door in the kitchen.	
8:00–8:15 p.m.	Call Mary to get a ride to the Senior Citizen Center for the community service activity. Check out driving arrangements.	
8:15–Bedtime	Relax!!!!! Listen to music, watch TV, go on the Internet, write in my journal. Set the alarm clock.	

student who has volunteered to help transfer students when she is uncertain how to proceed.

Whenever she needed to be reminded how to allocate her time, Erica referred to the pizza chart in the student handbook (Figure 3.4). Ms. Zuckerman, her new math teacher, used the diagram to illustrate how to begin the school year by focusing on what the student wants to achieve by the end of the school year. The pizza is a graphic reminder of how each month leads to academic success and graduation.

Consistent with the schoolwide goals for instructional time and safety, Ms. Zuckerman models the efficient use of her allocated class time for students. For example, five minutes before the period ends, she summarizes the important objectives achieved during the class by restating the relationship between individual student success and time management and by asking the students to name several ways they could use their understanding of the school year to better manage their time.

To model an effective use of time by teaching "bell to bell," Ms. Zuckerman involves students in learning activities from the beginning to the end of the class period. Her practices reflect the

---

Figure 3.4—Academic Year for Planning

Use the pieces of a pizza to visualize the eight, 5-week periods of the academic year and to plan for your success during each quarter.

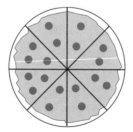

faculty consensus that today's higher state standards and more rigorous assessments create additional pressure to use every allocated instructional moment to engage students in learning. These instructional practices help the school achieve its goals for safety, student learning, and conduct by keeping students academically engaged until designated class-changing times. The administrative, guidance, and support staff also use these practices that promote safety and the continuity of instruction:

- Rotating guidance appointments and music lessons within a student's schedule to minimize the loss of instructional time in any one class
- Assessing, evaluating, and balancing the need for teachers to attend workshops, conferences, field trips, and meetings during scheduled class time against how the teacher's time out of the classroom affects student learning
- Eliminating field trips during the first month and last month of school and limiting them to one day a week
- Eliminating field trips and pull-out meetings and classes during intensive testing periods
- Eliminating the nonemergency use of the public address system during class periods
- Following a procedure developed by the teachers and administrators to limit the frequency and duration of student pull-out sessions for disciplinary actions

Mr. Sitran, Erica's guidance counselor, used these practices to arrange his first meeting with Erica. As she entered his office, Erica was surprised to see pictures of herself and other sophomores, taken during the orientation. Her schedule was in front of Mr. Sitran as he asked how she felt she was doing. He listened as Erica described how different Centerville is from her previous school and answered her questions about school rules and disciplinary procedures. Mr. Sitran scheduled a meeting for Erica and her parents to discuss three goals:

- Easing Erica's transition to her new school and community
- Designing her graduation and vocational plans
- Planning her parents' role in supporting Erica's efforts to achieve her goals.

Erica left the meeting feeling relieved that she could count on Mr. Sitran to help her succeed in school. Erica was not sure that she'd call any students on the volunteer list, but it was nice to have a formal way to contact peers to clarify the guidelines.

During the first month of school, the Centerville High School staff emphasized how to use RICE to manage the daily schedule, the academic calendar, and other issues that arise across grade levels and subject areas. In the process, staff members achieved their goals to increase instructional time and to support school safety.

The Third Month of School

During second period, Ms. Barett saw two students running down the corridor. As the hall monitor stopped the students, Ms. Barett recognized Brittany and Tara, seniors at Centerville High. Both students had a history of being late and cutting class.

"Good morning, Brittany and Tara. May I see your passes?"

"Hi, Ms. Barett. We were just on our way to class."

"Great! Let's walk together." As they walked and talked, Ms. Barett remembered that both girls had failed English language arts the previous year because they had cut class too often to complete the course requirements. As a result, they were taking two required classes of English language arts. As they approached their classroom, Ms. Barett gave each student a pass to meet with her individually during their sixth-period lunch. "Let's put a plan together so that we all enjoy that graduation day together! Tara, we'll get together at 12:10 in my office. Brittany, we'll see each other at 12:30."

Ms. Barett helped achieve school goals for instructional time and school safety by

- Supporting school procedures by asking the students for their passes
- Quickly bringing the students back to class
- Arranging to meet the students separately during noninstructional time
- Demonstrating RICE in her interactions with the students

When Ms. Barett met with Tara, they compared Tara's attendance pattern for the last quarter of the previous year with the first quarter of this year.

"Tara," she said, "do you notice a pattern?" She waited while Tara looked at the computer screen.

"I guess so."

"What is the pattern, Tara?"

"I cut English language arts when we have public speaking. I'm shy and hate to speak in front of others. I like it when we write. I just don't like to speak out loud."

"Tara," Ms. Barett responded, "it's really OK for you to like some activities more than others, but attending class is not negotiable. Right now, we have about 15 minutes to create a plan to help you earn the English credit you need to reach your goal of graduating with your class. So let's create a plan that I can help you with." Ms. Barett helped Tara create a plan based on RICE, as shown in Figure 3.5.

The corrective approach of working with a template and plan is an outgrowth of planning activities. The pupil personnel team identifies students with patterns of bullying, cutting class, attendance problems, other discipline concerns, and issues related to substance

Figure 3.5—RICE Strategy for Improving Student Attendance

Date: November 10
Student: Tara Moore
Administrator: Ms. Barett
Support Team Member: Mr. Howard, Counselor
Contact History Incident: Cutting Period 2   **Prior History:** Yes
Contact History Dates for This Incident: 11/10

Action:
• Meeting with administrator
• Developing a behavior replacement plan
• Sharing this incident and information with my guidance counselor and parents
• Being able to keep parking privileges if I keep this plan
• Having detention per school policy

Contact Progress and Status:
Pending follow-up on 11/12 and 11/13, and as needed

Goal	To attend all classes on time and graduate from high school
Current Behavior	Mostly attend only those classes I like
Resources	• Myself—Recognize why I'm cutting class • My friends—To help me attend every class and arrive on time. (Friends help friends get to every class on time!) • My guidance counselor or support staff—To help me use RICE to make good decisions • My parents or guardians—For advice, encouragement, and support
Obstacles	• My lack of impulse control • Peer pressure • Tempting situations, such as the cafeteria • Avoidance
Benchmarks	• Keeping track of class attendance in my student handbook • Completing my weekly progress sheet in the guidance office • Checking in with Ms. Barett for encouragement

_____   _____
Student's Signature   Administrator's Signature

abuse. The team also designs strategies for having identified students work with their counselors, parents, and other support staff to meet their goals for graduation and personal success.

As a result of the corrective and proactive strategies developed and implemented by the Centerville High School staff, the students are using formal classroom learning to make real-life decisions. They resist making short-term decisions that could have long-term negative consequences. Increasingly, students make the right decisions for the right reasons. Some students, however, have difficulty with impulse control and continue to make decisions for short-term gains, even at the cost of long-term negative consequences.

John's actions were typical for this particular group of students. Although he had studied RICE in his classes, he chose not to apply the principles when they interfered with his social needs, required him to ask for help, or compromised his image of having everything under control. John often used his social status to pressure other students to do his work. If students resisted, he bullied them, ridiculed them in public, threatened them in private, and maintained hostile behavior until they acquiesced. When Centerville High School adopted guiding principles, many students began to resist bullying. John found that getting peer support for his behavior became more difficult.

After an incident of cheating and related bullying behavior, John was referred to Ms. Barett. That same day, she met with him and asked what happened. Although John denied the allegations at first, Ms. Barett helped him feel comfortable enough to share his perceptions. She discovered how his feelings of test anxiety, anger, and fear led to his behavior. To transform those feelings into safe, appropriate actions, Ms. Barett asked John to use a scripting strategy to rewrite the incident with a guideline-driven focus. The goal of this activity was for John to create at least two options to use when he feels anxious, angry, or afraid.

With John's involvement each step of the way, Ms. Barett also met with his counselor and parents. Together, they created a behavior replacement plan that identified John's bullying and cheating behaviors and invoked consequences consistent with school policy. In Centerville High School, the range of consequences include in-school suspension, out-of-school suspension, loss of parking privileges, and loss of senior privileges. Supports were put into place to help John implement his behavior replacement plan so that he could begin to apply RICE in his everyday decision making.

The counselor used the pizza chart in the student handbook to remind John that it was early in the year and that he had three marking periods left to be successful. At the end of the students' school day and before the start of extracurricular activities and sports practice, Ms. Barett met with John's teachers to help everyone understand that John was concerned about his grades and that he needed extra help to catch up. The counselor worked with Ms. Barett to monitor John's progress and kept his parents informed once a week.

School staff know the importance of including a component to sustain John's behavior replacement plan before and after school vacations, because vacations can distract from the school routine. The staff identified these periods as opportunities to use RICE to continue the instructional focus within the school and to extend learning at home and in the community. As part of the effort, the Centerville staff and students use the academic calendar and daily schedule to increase instructional time and to enhance school and community safety. The Centerville High School Safe Halloween Program is one example of how the school community demonstrates RICE by inviting elementary and prekindergarten students to visit the high school to "trick or treat" in a safe environment. High school students volunteer to decorate rooms and to entertain. Much of this work is done through clubs or class activities, but several teachers also devote limited classroom time to Halloween literature and history, which the high school students share with the younger students who attend the event. This after-school activity has several purposes:

- Providing high-school students with opportunities to serve as role models to the younger students and to interact with the community in a positive setting
- Letting the younger students "trick or treat" in a safe and secure environment
- Extending instructional time as high school students read Halloween stories and write poems with elementary students
- Offering a social service by reducing the number of pranks and the vandalism normally associated with Halloween, thereby demonstrating impulse control and respect (many of the volunteers are potential pranksters)

Exam Time

John couldn't believe that he had reached the end of the first semester. Half the year was over—half the "pizza" in his student handbook was gone. He had been following the behavior replacement plan he put together with Ms. Barett and his guidance counselor, and he was about to find out whether all that hard work had paid off. Midterm exams were about to begin.

At a pupil personnel team meeting, the guidance counselor and Ms. Barett commented that John had consistently followed his behavior replacement plan. The progress reports that his teachers had submitted indicated that his impulse control was measurably improved (see Appendix C for a template). The team agreed that John had benefited from regularly scheduled support. That ongoing support would continue to be especially important during the midyear testing period, given John's past difficulties with preparing for tests.

Before Centerville High School implemented the guiding principles approach, the midyear testing period was often fraught with conflicts and time pressures for the entire student population and staff. Using information from needs assessment and input from parents and students, the faculty and administrative team created a midyear testing structure with the following features:

• Exams are scheduled within class periods, which results in increased instructional time and no disruption of school routine.

• All students either attend class or take exams during the school day. No student has unallocated instructional time. As a result, the students do not wander the halls or the community.

• In class, students develop individual and peer plans to succeed during the testing period. Teachers, during the summer workshops, learned how to help students create these study-group models in all academic areas. Like the staff who use collegial circles within the building to support continual professional development, the students meet in groups after school, during study hall, or at lunch to help one another study and succeed in academic endeavors.

• The *Chronicle* publishes a supplement notifying parents of testing schedules and offering them tips to help their children succeed.

At a faculty meeting, two teachers described an approach to proctoring that they use to create a positive climate. They suggest a logical sequence of steps to save time and reduce stress:

• Ensure acquisition of all supplies necessary for administering the test.

• Get to the test site before the students, and ensure that the site is orderly and welcoming.

- Check the list of students who are assigned to the site.
- Check the list of students who require test modifications.
- Set, explain, and ensure students follow test distribution and collection procedures.
- Check that each student understands the test directions before leaving the area where the tests are picked up.
- Stay sensitive to student needs, such as the importance of students' knowing how much time remains at specific intervals.

The faculty found this presentation so rewarding that they decided to revisit the proctoring process during a professional development workshop on assessment and grading. Their priority was to evaluate and modify, as needed, the proctoring approach for midyear tests so that they could better prepare students for final exams. The teachers agreed to incorporate test-preparation strategies into their instructional, counseling, and discipline activities throughout the month.

This process of linking professional development to professional practice was an outgrowth of the first workshop on guiding principles. The professional staff continually asked, "What can we do to make this school an inviting, orderly place for each student?" Another example of connecting workshops to professional practice was the staff response to the results of the Exit Survey of Graduating Seniors (see Appendix D). The guidance department prepared the survey and subsequent professional development workshops because of its interest in student needs, especially during the senior year.

The senior survey produced both positive and negative feedback from the students. On the positive side, seniors conducted key activities for their peers, especially younger students, and were instrumental in fostering student support for the guiding principles approach. One criticism emerged about the school calendar. Seniors felt that the scheduling process outlined in the school calendar made course selection confusing and stressful. As a result, students made impulsive or uninformed decisions about their schedules without clearly understanding the ramifications of their choices. The staff believed that students would benefit from a planning process that would help them use RICE to make course selections on the basis of the following criteria:

- The purpose of school
- Graduation requirements
- Their role as a student
- The role of the guidance counselor as a resource

The results from the survey of staff (see Appendix E) confirmed the belief that the course selection process was confusing and stressful. The survey explored four areas of concerns to students, parents, and staff: scheduling, making connections with others, having opportunities to develop abilities and interests, and planning for postsecondary life. The results indicated that teachers, administrators, and counselors also believed that the scheduling process, among other things, could be improved. Specifically, they cited high numbers of schedule changes being requested by students at the beginning of the school year, especially related to student requests to have or not have certain teachers just before and after school opened.

The staff used the results of these surveys as well as random interviews with students to revamp the course offerings and scheduling calendar. The goal was to create a scheduling process that was clear, effective, and aligned with the guiding principles. The staff made scheduling a structured, real-life, decision-making lesson in which all students could apply the principles of RICE to achieve their goals. The school now uses the guiding principles approach for course selection and scheduling by opening Course Selection and Scheduling Month with a series of grade-level assembly programs.

During these assemblies, the staff illustrate the major steps of making successful course selections.

The process of selecting courses and scheduling is now aligned with the instructional, counseling, and discipline goals and standards adopted by Centerville High School. Counselors help seniors develop transition plans for college, career, and independent living. The counselors for the other grades help students create schedules for the next year of high school. The most significant changes to the course selection and scheduling process include

- Revising the procedure to add, delete, or modify courses. During summer workshops, faculty evaluate courses to ensure that they are aligned with state standards and assessments. At joint faculty-student meetings held twice a year, students offer suggestions and help ensure that the principles of RICE are incorporated into the course content in ways that are meaningful to them.
- Reworking the course descriptions and booklet to ensure that the language and organization are clear and reflect the guiding principles. The faculty and student council representatives collaborated on the effort. For example, the students made technology suggestions that might not have occurred to the staff. As a result, the high school webmaster added a section to the school's home page so that students and parents could see course descriptions and have access to the necessary forms at home.
- Conducting a timely, informative assembly program to help students connect graduation requirements to their individual course selections. Guidance staff work with administrators, teachers, parents, and elected class officers to design and conduct the assembly.
- Meeting with a guidance counselor to incorporate information from the student handbook along with personal information such as results of midterm exams, midyear grades, career goals, teacher input, and personal issues to construct a proposed typical day and homework load.

• Supporting student and parent understanding of the goals, roles, and scheduling implications of academic intervention services. Counselors provide support to students as they make the transitions into and out of such services.

• Supporting and monitoring seniors and juniors through individual and small-group sessions consistent with the National Standards for School Counseling Programs. Counselors give frequent and intensive guidance contact to students who feel conflicted or overwhelmed by the prospect of leaving high school.

The counselors and other Centerville High School staff expect the reorganized course listing and scheduling calendar to reduce or eliminate many of the concerns cited by the students and staff. After completing the course selection and scheduling process for the coming year, the staff and students turned their attention to using the academic calendar and daily schedule to maintain instructional focus and safety in the final months of school.

End-of-Year Activities

Mr. Spitzer, the high school principal, called a meeting following the awards assemblies and graduation activities at the end of the first full year of using the guiding principles. At this meeting, the Centerville High School administrators, teachers, and student representatives identified three key areas to be aligned with the guiding principles approach in the coming year: selecting and presenting students with awards, incorporating senior activities into the regular school day by maintaining a clear instructional focus, and improving the graduation ceremony.

Each area was identified through the original needs assessment completed by the staff. The senior survey also indicated that many students felt left out of senior activities, including awards nights and proms. For example, during Bret's three years at Centerville High, he volunteered at the Centerville Senior Center, where he worked with senior citizens during recreational activities and holiday cele- brations. As president of the Students Against Drunk Driving (SADD) chapter, he organized fund-raising activities to help provide food and clothes for families in need within the community. In those years, his friends were given awards for academic and athletic excellence, but Bret was not recognized for his contributions to the community. To align the awards with the guiding principles, the high school's awards committee now uses new criteria and proce- dures to recognize students, such as Bret, who would have been overlooked.

The awards process now begins when the principal requests nominations for students who should be recognized for service. These nominations may be from community organizations, business groups, and agencies involved with Centerville High School. The principal invites elementary and middle school teachers and admin- istrators, as well as representatives of local community agencies and businesses, to attend the awards assembly and to present awards. Students established criteria for Centerville Hero Awards, which they give to a staff member at each grade level who personifies the guiding principles of RICE. Faculty established criteria and give sim- ilar awards to a student at each grade level who personifies the guid- ing principles. By recognizing Bret and many other students for their service to the community, a more meaningful connection is made between school and community life for students, their parents, and the community.

Just as awards assemblies were restructured to be more inclusive, meaningful, and aligned with the guiding principles initiative, so were all the senior year activities. Staff members wanted the stu- dents to approach their senior year as an opportunity to apply the principles of RICE to their decisions about current and future roles, goals, and responsibilities. Staff members also wanted to ensure that school rules, routines, and instructional focus were consistently maintained for all students from the first day of class through graduation, regardless of celebrations and events.

In this context, the staff understood that the seniors wanted to celebrate their accomplishments during their culminating year at Centerville High School. They decided that this need to celebrate presented seniors with an opportunity to fulfill their role as citizens. They developed a variety of strategies to help the students in this process:

• The senior portfolio project: Seniors in the Civics and Government class completed a portfolio with evidence of RICE-related activities focused on improving their community.

• Mentorship program: Centerville students became either mentors or mentees in the school or in the community. For example, high school students served as big brothers or big sisters to teach elementary school students how to resolve conflicts peacefully.

• Senior advisory: Faculty and staff members serve as advisors to small groups of seniors to monitor, support, and encourage them, thereby reducing alienation, isolation, truancy, anonymity, and failure to graduate. The advisors worked with groups of four students, meeting with them once a week for 15 minutes at the end of the school day, before extracurricular activities and sports practice.

• Reallocation of staff time and activities: Members of the administrative, faculty, and support teams took up visible positions during times of high stress. For example, two days before vacation periods, staff and administrators followed their plan to be more visible in the halls and around the entrances and exits.

• A new look for the prom: A core group of staff, students, and parents restructured the prom by addressing financial factors, increasing student participation, increasing inclusiveness, and strengthening character and conduct. Character and conduct were addressed through several activities: offering positive peer support through SADD; relating short-term decisions to long-term goals; and involving parents in supporting responsible, alcohol-free and other drug-free activities before and after the prom.

The staff recognized that culminating activities evoke conflicting feelings for seniors, their parents, and some staff members. No school event arouses more powerful emotions than graduation. The Centerville High School staff and students recognized the need for a plan to ensure that graduation day was congruent with the philosophy of RICE for all participants.

On the basis of staff and parent evaluations regarding the previous year's graduation day, the commencement planning team developed a comprehensive commencement program that focused on shared goals, specific roles, and the guiding principles of RICE. As a first step, faculty and administrators established the criteria for senior participation in graduation exercises: Given the shared purpose of school and the rigorous learning standards, only those students who have successfully met all graduation requirements can participate.

The next task was to work out the details for the graduation ceremony. The senior advisor and the administrative team collaborated to set standards and procedures to ensure that themes, speeches, speakers, and musical programs reflected the guiding principles of RICE. The school safety committee, comprising administrators, teachers, the school nurse, security personnel, and students, created a plan to provide a safe and orderly graduation day centered on RICE, with special emphasis on respect and impulse control.

As with many schools, seating at end-of-year ceremonies is limited; therefore students, staff, and parents met to establish criteria for equitably distributing tickets. It was decided that any extra tick-

---

Figure 3.6—Using the Calendar with Elementary and Middle School Students

Use the school calendar to plan important events and schedule time to prepare students for their next steps in their educational journey.

Elementary school
- Elementary classroom teachers and administrators collaborate to preserve the integrity of instructional time by establishing uninterrupted reading and math blocks during which no pull-outs are permitted.
- Fifth grade teachers help students use their student handbooks to predict and plan what an average school day in middle school will be like.
- Moving-up exercises are organized to be inclusive and to demonstrate the principles of RICE. A parent, faculty, and administrative planning team establishes guidelines for all adults and students to follow during these events.

Middle school
- Middle school administrators and teachers eliminate field trips during the first and last months of school and during intensive testing periods to preserve the integrity of instructional time.
- Middle school students visit the high school and shadow 9th grade students for one day as part of their orientation to high school.
- Students and their parents participate in joint workshops to explore graduation requirements and to create daily academic schedules for their freshman year of high school.

---

ets would be distributed through a lottery system. In addition, the planning team arranged for people with special needs to be safely transported from parking areas to appropriate seating.

In a special supplement of the *Centerville High School Chronicle*, the senior advisor, the senior class president, the principal, and the high school Parent-Teacher Association (PTA) president published an article outlining how parents, graduates, and guests can use the guiding principles of RICE to ensure that they fulfill their respective roles at graduation.

Recognizing that commencement is as much a beginning as an end, Mr. Spitzer, his administrative team, and student representatives agreed that their graduation ceremony was as much a part of the academic program as it was a part of the counseling and discipline programs. Graduation planning became a vehicle for instruction, counseling, and proactive planning for appropriate conduct, including respect, impulse control, compassion, and equity. Staff, students, and parents helped create a graduation ceremony that reflected academic excellence, citizenship, and support for students.

Through the awards-related activities and graduation ceremonies, the students learn that the way they make transitions in school can serve as a model for their transitions throughout the rest of their academic, professional, and personal lives.

This chapter focused on how a high school used the daily schedule and academic calendar to improve student learning, character, and conduct. Figure 3.6 lists some ways elementary and middle school educators can use daily schedules and academic calendars to accomplish similar goals.

4

Hallways and Bus Stops

Twelve-year-old Lauren couldn't wait to tell Nicole what Robbie had said about her on the telephone last night. When Lauren had called Nicole, her dad replied that Nicole had to study for a test, and her dad wouldn't let her use the phone. Now Nicole wanted to hear all the news. "What did he say about me?" Lauren laughed and raced down the hall to her locker. "C'mere, C'mere, Nikki. I'll tell you!" she yelled as she pushed through the crowd and accidentally bumped into Ms. Kurtz, the hall monitor. "Good morning, Lauren. May I help you? You seem to be in such a rush." "Oh, I'm sorry, Ms. Kurtz. I didn't see you! Nicole's chasing me. Nicole, say you're sorry to Ms. Kurtz!"

Smiling, Ms. Kurtz quietly asked the girls to join her near the lockers, out of the way of the traffic, and shared her concerns for their safety as well as that of other students. "Lauren and Nicole, I'll bet that you had something important to say to each other. But you did push into a lot of people. How will you get to your lockers the next time?" Nicole apologized and said that she would walk quickly instead of running, even when she really wanted to rush. Lauren agreed and said that she would tell Nicole any news on the bus, instead of teasing and waiting and running ahead. Ms. Kurtz thanked them for using the principles of RICE—respect, impulse control, compassion, and equity—to make better decisions and said that she was looking forward to seeing them later that day. Lauren and Nicole giggled and walked quickly to their lockers, sharing their news about Robbie.

As Ms. Kurtz walked back to her post, she thought, "What a difference a year makes." Last year, before the entire school staff adopted the guiding principles approach, this small incident could easily have escalated into a bigger problem, and she would have handled it differently. Instead, she helped create an opportunity for students to apply RICE to real-life situations in the halls of Centerville Middle School. At that moment, Mrs. Carter, the assistant principal, stopped just long enough to say, "Nice job, Ms. Kurtz."

Everyone involved in this incident felt good about the outcome. The monitor positively engaged the students, stayed within her assigned area, remained within her role, and used her skills to prevent conflicts that often erupt in hallways. The students recognized the RICE language from the lessons they learned in their courses. They demonstrated respect for their own role as well as for the role of the monitor, and they moved quickly to their assigned classes. The assistant principal gave the staff member immediate and positive feedback and was pleased that a potentially inflammatory incident had been averted. By taking these actions, the monitor, the students, and the assistant principal all advanced the shared purpose of the school: To promote student learning and school safety.

Ms. Kurtz used strategies she had learned in the staff development workshops during the previous school year. Custodians, hall monitors, clerical staff, cafeteria workers, security personnel, and other noninstructional members of the Centerville Middle School staff participated in these same workshops. Like the workshops conducted separately for bus drivers during conference days, these sessions were designed to help participants

  • Identify the shared purpose of school as a place to help students learn and stay safe
  • Clarify their own role in helping the school fulfill that purpose

• Affirm that their role includes establishing supportive connections with students, and

    • Practice strategies to use RICE to engage students appropriately.

This chapter illustrates two major points: All staff can use noninstructional settings as a natural extension of the written curriculum and instructional focus. School staff can use noninstructional
settings to help students apply guiding principles in settings where
students move more freely, adult supervision is less direct, and no
formal academic tasks are involved.

Hallways

The Centerville Middle School faculty, staff, parents, and students
consider hallway behavior an important element of the school curriculum. In the hallways, students have the opportunity to apply the
guiding principles as they interact with one another, with teachers,
and with other adults in an informal and supportive way. The hallways offer students a unique mix of instruction, counsel, and discipline. They function as environments that help students better
understand themselves, secure a place of importance in their peer
group, and make appropriate contact with adults.

In previous years, student behavior in the hallways included
running, pushing, cursing, and shouting to kissing, fighting, and bullying. Students saw the hallways as places to cut class, harass schoolmates, and avoid adults. Between classes, the teachers and administrators were generally in their classrooms or offices. The monitors
and security guards often congregated in corners with one another
or with a handful of students. The staff voiced concerns about students being late to class, showing disrespect, and often entering class
in an agitated mood in response to a hallway incident. These concerns were raised at monthly meetings of the school safety team.

This group of administrators, teachers, noninstructional staff, parents, and students recommended that all stakeholders, including students, should apply the guiding principles in the way they fulfill their respective roles in the hallways:

- Students fulfill their role by moving quickly and safely to their destinations and by interacting appropriately with others.
- Teachers fulfill their role by being visible outside their classrooms or in other assigned locations during class changes. In this role, the teachers monitor student behavior and interact with students, thereby promoting school safety.
- Administrators fulfill their role by actively monitoring and engaging students in the hallways and in other noninstructional areas of the building.
- Monitors and security guards fulfill their role by actively observing students and adults, by communicating with others as needed, and by helping students move quickly and safely to their destinations.
- Parents fulfill their role by following school procedures for visitors and by encouraging their children to use the guiding principles throughout the day.

The Centerville Middle School faculty, staff, students, and parents adopted the team's recommendations. As a result, all stakeholders began to appreciate how such noninstructional settings as hallways provide opportunities to apply the guiding principles to achieve goals about student learning and school safety. The hallway is now intentionally used as a component of the curriculum.

On her way to her physical education class, Nicole exchanged greetings with several staff members in the hallway and reminded a friend to save a seat for her at lunch. As she entered class, she saw the athletic director and the teacher organizing students into teams to brainstorm solutions to a current problem: students sharing lockers, losing property, and violating school policies and procedures for locker safety.

Lockers

The athletic director, Mr. Bracken, started the class by reading the highlights of a letter he received at a recent PTA meeting:

> I am writing to ask for your help. My daughter and her friend share a locker and now all its contents are missing, including a special bracelet given to my daughter by her grandmother. This is the second time that my daughter's property has disappeared this school year. I am writing to inform you of this problem and to say that I expect property to be safe when it's in a locker at school. I expect this problem will be solved.

After reading this letter aloud, Mr. Bracken helped the group reach agreement with the parent. The teacher paraphrased their shared view by stating that "we all expect property to be safe in our school. We all have a role in using RICE to achieve our shared goals to learn well and to stay safe."

Mr. Bracken quickly focused the group on strategies that each person could use to fulfill a role in creating and maintaining a safe and secure school environment. In this way, he transformed the problem into a decision-making opportunity. He posed the following three questions, and students worked in their teams to develop their suggestions, which were shared at the next school safety team meeting.

• If a student asks you to share your locker, what are two things you can say or do to follow locker procedures and cope with peer pressure?

• If you see or hear of a student opening a locker that isn't her own, breaking into lockers, or stealing property, which adult in the school would you involve and what would you say?

• If you see or hear that someone has brought to school an illegal substance, a weapon, or some other item not permitted on school grounds, which adult in the school would you involve and what would you say?

At the end of this lesson, Mr. Bracken and the physical education teacher, Mr. Chi, collected the materials and shared key results with the students. Although the students offered many appropriate suggestions, the most frequently mentioned response to the first question was that alternatives do exist and that students would like some training in face-saving techniques for dealing with peer pressure. This problem-solving experience was a success because it offered developmentally appropriate decision-making opportunities for middle school students to apply the guiding principles to better understand themselves and their actions.

Over the next two weeks, Mr. Bracken shared the results of the brainstorming session with the members of the administrative council, who agreed that the entire faculty and the school safety team should receive the same information. One short-term outcome of this learning activity was the school safety team's recommendation that three monitors be assigned to physical education locker room areas for the first and last seven minutes of each class period. Two long-term outcomes followed. First, the administrators, teachers, pupil personnel, and students taught students how to reach out for appropriate adult support. Second, adults participated in professional development activities to learn how to connect with middle school students in receptive and responsive ways. In response to the parent who wrote the letter, Mr. Bracken shared the variety of ways the school had addressed her concerns and invited her to attend the next PTA meeting, which was to focus on the parent's role in promoting school safety.

The need to provide appropriate adult support is an issue for all noninstructional areas. The Centerville Middle School cafeteria incorporates adult support into activities that are interesting to students and related to the goals of the school.

Cafeteria

As Nicole entered the cafeteria, her friend Susann called out, "I saved your seat!" Nicole nodded and waved and joined the salad line. The salad line and two other food stations are a new way the cafeteria is able to offer a menu that appeals to students and satisfies federal requirements for school lunches, while improving the flow of student traffic and reducing wait time.

In previous years, members of the school community had identified the student cafeteria as a noninstructional area where students were cutting class, fighting, behaving disrespectfully, throwing food, and engaging in other behaviors that threatened school safety and security. The adults who worked in the cafeteria felt unappreciated. They were often the target of complaints by parents, students, and staff. When students were referred to administrators for disciplinary infractions, they complained about the way the adults and other students interacted in the cafeteria. A cafeteria committee of staff, students, the food service director, representatives of the school, and lunch room monitors met four times over the course of a year to align cafeteria practices and procedures with the guiding principles. They put into place the following goals and actions:

• To reduce wait time and increase speed of purchase, three specialized, fast-moving food stations have replaced the single line for all food purchases.
• To improve safety, conduct, and communications within the cafeteria, students and staff apply the guiding principles to all cir-

cumstances, including when they feel frustrated, anxious, or angry. Adults are interspersed appropriately throughout the cafeteria so that they can make positive connections with students in a relaxed and supportive way.

• To make the cafeteria a more welcoming environment, student-created murals and posters that illustrate the guiding principles of RICE in the cafeteria decorate the walls. Students and staff fulfill their roles to keep the cafeteria clean and orderly. The art class designed a new weekly menu, which is posted outside the cafeteria and on the school's Web page.

• To improve the use of time in the cafeteria, selected student service personnel are available during lunch periods, including guidance counselors, social workers, drug counselors, club advisors, and peer mediation leaders. Teachers and students' peers offer extra academic help and tutoring. Preliminary college and career planning activities, appropriate to middle school students, are available and include videoclips, print materials, guest speakers, and demonstrations.

Seventh graders Nicole and Susann quickly finish eating and move to the extra-help table where they tutor 6th grade students in math. In a semiprivate corner of the cafeteria, their friend Lauren talks with her guidance counselor about some difficulty she is having with another student.

These students use their time productively because the entire cafeteria program is structured to help the school achieve its learning and safety goals. As a result of careful, goal-oriented planning, professional development, and student involvement, the cafeteria is another noninstructional area where staff apply the curriculum and the schoolwide instructional focus to help students develop and apply character and conduct skills.

Conference days now include workshops for cafeteria staff to brainstorm and practice using the guiding principles to fulfill their role in relation to the school's safety and learning goals. The cafeteria staff understand how they affect student behavior in the cafeteria and feel supported by the entire school community.

The cafeteria is a unique noninstructional setting, in that time and space are available to meet student needs without interrupting instructional time or keeping students after school. The staff and students of Centerville Middle School have transformed the normative structure of the cafeteria and have improved both learning and school safety in the process.

Restrooms

As Nicole walked quickly to the nurse's office to use the restroom that all the girls call "the clean one," she made a mental note to raise the cleanliness issue at her student advisory meeting that afternoon. Nicole, Lauren, and many of their friends, both male and female, had observed the following behaviors and conditions in student restrooms:

- Lack of supervision
- Students smoking cigarettes and using controlled substances
- Students cutting class
- Intimidation and bullying
- Inadequate supplies
- Vandalism and graffiti
- Dirty conditions and poor maintenance
- Door locks or entire doors missing
- Lack of regard for human dignity

Students, staff, and parents expressed many concerns about these conditions. At a special meeting of the Centerville Middle School student advisory council, administrators, faculty leaders, the school nurse, and parents joined with students to consider how to extend the guiding principles into daily practices associated with student restrooms. In the course of this and subsequent meetings, students and staff worked together to create an action plan that included a time line. They organized the action plan around the roles of the individual members of the group; each member had a specific series of tasks to complete within the given time frame.

For example, the administrators were responsible for three major activities: scheduling and supervising the adults stationed outside all open restrooms and ensuring that school procedures are followed; conducting a cost-benefit analysis comparing the costs and benefits of increasing staff to monitor restrooms with the costs of vandalism, repairs, maintenance, and negative public image; and supervising appropriate custodial staff to follow proper restroom maintenance routines and standards of cleanliness.

The students took responsibility for a range of actions: implementing a schoolwide health information campaign linking the guiding principles to behaviors that promote health and safety in the restrooms; encouraging students to use the guiding principles to protect school property, use basic restroom etiquette, and respond appropriately to adult supervision of restroom facilities; and collaborating with the art and health teachers to provide informative, supportive, and attractive art for the restrooms.

Parents agreed to help their children use the guiding principles to take personal responsibility for their actions in the restrooms and throughout the school. In addition, parents supported an initiative for a capital-improvement project to update Centerville Middle School restrooms.

Teachers agreed to take immediate steps: to routinely walk into the restrooms; to respond promptly when they become aware of rumors about, or evidence of, problem behavior in the restrooms; and to follow school procedures for referring all such problems.

The school nurse agreed to fulfill her role to provide comprehensive school health education. Many students make connections with the school nurse because her noninstructional, supportive setting offers students relief from the pressures that surround them. Ms. Laurette, the school nurse, uses these opportunities to help students use the guiding principles to cope with their everyday stresses and to follow school procedures to get the help they need.

Clinic

When Nicole and Susann arrived at their sixth-period math class, Ben was already seated, directly behind them. Instead of greeting them as he normally did, Ben seemed to ignore them. Susann tried to get his attention by smiling and turning around quickly to look at him. Nothing worked. Susann even thought that he was saying things about her to Rosalie. Susann wanted to cry but was afraid that the others would see her. "What's the matter?" Nicole whispered. Susann shook her head and covered her face with her hands. As Mr. Marks walked past her, Susann told him that she felt sick and needed a pass to the clinic. Although Susann knew that she should not leave the math class, especially because they were reviewing for tomorrow's test, she felt that hiding her emotions from the class was more important. Mr. Marks handed her the pass, and Susann cried as she walked to the clinic.

Ms. Laurette, the school nurse, invited Susann to sit by her desk and inquired about her symptoms. Susann continued to cry as she explained how she felt about the way Ben treated her. Ms. Laurette listened compassionately and affirmed how upsetting it can be when we think that people we care about are ignoring us. As Susann regained composure, they worked together to help Susann review her behavior. For example, she recognized a pattern of leaving class and coming to the clinic when she was upset. Susann agreed to use impulse control to cope with her emotions so that she could focus on her work. She also agreed to meet with the guidance counselor to develop a plan to handle her emotions. Ms. Laurette encouraged

Susann to come to her office just to say hello and to touch base on her way out of the building each day—when she has time.

When Susann left, Ms. Laurette called Susann's guidance counselor and shared her concerns about Susann's pattern of leaving class and visiting the clinic. They agreed that Susann would benefit from a plan to help her use impulse control more effectively and consistently. When Susann returned to class, she quietly asked Nicole for the review notes she missed during the few minutes she had been away. At the end of the period, Mr. Marks dropped into the clinic to check with Ms. Laurette about Susann. He agreed with Ms. Laurette's assessment of Susann's pattern of behavior and indicated that he would monitor her requests for passes.

This scenario illustrates how each stakeholder used the guiding principles to fulfill a role in the schoolwide effort to help students focus on learning and feeling safe. Susann asked for appropriate adult support instead of getting involved in an argument with Ben or acting out in class. Mr. Marks communicated with the nurse, who in turn accomplished three goals: (1) she fostered a positive connection with a student in need; (2) she helped Susann regain her composure so that she could return to class quickly; and (3) she referred Susann to a guidance counselor for support.

Consistent with the school's goal to improve the use of time by offering planned activities during students' lunch periods, Susann's guidance counselor met with her the next day in the cafeteria. Over several weeks, Susann gradually eliminated her visits to the nurse during class time. As Ms. Laurette suggested, Susann occasionally stops by the nurse's office after school.

At the end of the day, Susann, Nicole, Robbie, and Ben passed each other in the bus parking lot and joked as they boarded buses to go home. The Centerville staff views the bus area as another place to exercise the guiding principles because it presents many opportunities for the staff to make individual connections with students and enhance student safety.

Buses

In previous years, the Centerville Middle School staff found that many problems stemmed from the conflicts that occurred in the bus area during arrival and dismissal times. Staff, bus drivers, parents, and students lodged complaints about fighting, bullying, name calling, pushing, and vandalism. In addition, students and staff were placed in jeopardy by adults who ignored laws, district policies, and school procedures for driving and parking on school grounds and for picking up and dropping off students. Often, unattended vehicles prevented buses from entering or exiting in a safe and timely fashion. These problems undermined school safety and interfered with instructional time.

During the annual review of the Centerville Middle School's safety plan, the administrative team determined that the parking area offered opportunities for applying the guiding principles of respect, impulse control, compassion, and equity, as did the other noninstructional settings. Following the approach used to reorganize the cafeteria, the team set the following key goals and completed or supported the following actions:

• To improve safety, conduct, and communication in the bus and parking areas, the school community publicized the existing laws, district policies, and school procedures to each group of stakeholders. The administrators addressed the PTA; the principal included information in the monthly newsletter; the school newspaper featured a story with tips for parents; the Community Oriented Policing Enforcement (COPE) officer helped the students understand their role in promoting their own safety and that of others in all traffic-related areas, including the school bus area; the Centerville Teacher's Association included a related update in its monthly newsletter; and the student government led a poster campaign with the art club to remind students to follow the bus area safety procedures. The school also provided stakeholder groups with feedback indicating the results of the bus and parking area safety initiative.

• To make the bus and parking areas safe, school personnel followed traffic and safety standards for painting and maintaining demarcation lines, and they posted and maintained traffic signs. They also installed signs welcoming students, parents, and other community members to school, thereby extending the theme of safe schools to the parking lot and the community. School staff enforced laws, policies, and procedures consistently. The administration reas-signed security and other staff to ensure safety and to improve con-nections between students and school staff. For example, security and other staff refer to students by name, use standard greetings, and model other respectful interactions that set a positive tone at the beginning and the end of each school day.

• To reduce wait time for students as they prepare to exit or enter buses or cars safely, and for buses and cars to exit or enter the premises safely, security and other school staff make contact with stu-dents while encouraging them to enter or exit the school quickly. Bus traffic and automobile traffic were separated to improve traffic flow; to increase safety; and to help bus drivers, parents, and other adults model appropriate behaviors consistent with the guiding principles.

The buses and parking areas offer unique opportunities to pro-mote the guiding principles across the school community because every student and staff member experiences the rituals of arrival and departure. The Centerville Middle School arrival and departure pro-cedures encourage students and staff to feel part of a safe and welcom-ing community and help them fulfill their roles. Because parents and other adults have a more active role in this setting than in any other school-based location, Centerville parents needed to understand that their decisions to follow laws and procedures in the parking lot help their children follow rules and procedures throughout the day.

Through a series of workshops conducted on conference days throughout the year, bus drivers established a new connection between their role with the students and the goals of the school. They learned how to use the guiding principles to communicate with students, parents, and staff and how to fulfill their role. They felt less isolated and more supported in their own efforts to promote safety and to interact with students in their daily routines.

Figure 4.1—Using Guiding Principles in Noninstructional Settings

Elementary school

Playground: Elementary classroom teachers, administrators, and monitors collaborate to help students apply the guiding principles to prevent or resolve the conflicts that develop when children are engaged in play activities during recess.

Cafeteria: Older students serve as buddies to younger students during lunch periods. This buddy system includes helping with homework, reading aloud, and other natural opportunities to make connections, engage in appropriate behavior, and model the guiding principles in action.

Buses: Students sit in assigned seats on the buses so that fewer conflicts develop. Bus drivers are given bus seating charts that include students' pictures and names. With this information, the bus driver can identify and greet the children by name and can protect the children from accidentally taking the wrong bus. The students also know the name of the bus driver.

High school

Cafeteria: Students have opportunities to interact with guidance and other pupil personnel staff. In addition, centers for career and college fairs are offered, along with tables for peer tutoring, language immersion activities, contemporary issues discussion groups led by staff, and clubs.

Parking: Students qualify for a parking permit by following school rules and procedures and demonstrating the principles of RICE.

Assemblies: All students and adults use the guiding principles to demonstrate audience skills consistent with their respective roles in the school community. For example, administrators, teachers, and pupil personnel sit among students and model appropriate audience behavior. Parents stay for the entire program or performance. Students applaud appropriately for all performers. All audience members are quiet during programs and performances.

By taking a comprehensive approach to bus and parking area safety, all members of the Centerville Middle School community help students learn and stay safe. The faculty and staff find that their use of the guiding principles to engage and supervise students in the bus area sets a welcoming tone. The students enter and exit the building and buses in a safer, respectful, and orderly way. In addition, students arrive at class on time and ready to learn, and the staff on duty find that students behave more appropriately than before.

The experiences of Nicole, her friends, and the Centerville Middle School community illustrate how students and staff can use noninstructional areas and activities to achieve goals for learning and school safety. Figure 4.1 offers tips for how elementary school and high school educators can use noninstructional settings and the hidden curriculum to promote school goals.

5

Play Ball: Student Athletics

Coach Noel called the players together the day before the last home football game of the regular season. Everyone knew that Centerville already had a top seed in the upcoming playoffs; they also knew that the last home game would be against Madison. The coach knew that the game would not affect the standings and understood that the game would produce life-long memories for the players and their families. Coach Noel wanted to give every senior, especially those with little playing time during the season, the dream of their high school career: to start in the final home game of the season.

With these thoughts in mind, Coach Noel shared the game plan with the team. The game plan reflects his way of showing Centerville High School's appreciation for the commitment and sacrifice that all the players had made over the years. Coach Noel shared that the game plan would recognize that the entire team had given up family vacations and other social opportunities for practice sessions and games, with little free time for a regular social life. He affirmed how consistently the second string had supported the first-string players and how the first string had appreciated their efforts. Now the second-string seniors would have their chance to invite family and friends to see them start in their final home game of their high school career.

After hearing the game plan, Keith couldn't wait to get home and tell his parents that he would be starting in tomorrow's game. "Hey, Mom! Don't be late to the game tomorrow," Keith called out as he entered the house. "Coach says I'm starting, and everybody's walking me across the field with the other seniors!"

"Everybody? Who's everybody?" his brother Eddie shouted back.

"You, Eddie. And Mom and Dad. Everybody in the family. Coach calls it Senior Day. He saw it at a college game. The family walks the senior athlete across the field before the game starts, and everybody applauds. It's the first time at Centerville, but now it's our tradition, too."

After Keith's mother hugged and congratulated him, she and Keith's father got the cameras ready for the big day and called family and friends to make sure that they would arrive at the game on time. They asked their friends to save them a seat where Keith could see them easily from the field.

Through the thoughts and reflections of stakeholders who directly or indirectly influence the Centerville High School athletic program, we can focus on the important aspects of the final football game of the season to illustrate how this high school has

- Reevaluated how the athletic program is an extension of the larger school program
- Recognized that the athletic program is a unique driving force for many members of the school community to connect with one another, with the school, and with sports
- Affirmed that the athletic program creates many opportunities to strengthen connections between parents and children
- Validated how the ideals of athleticism and sportsmanship express the Centerville School District's commitment to excellence in learning and safety

The Athletic Program

High school athletic programs can be a powerful way to involve parents in the school community. Recognizing this power, the athletic directors and coaches at Centerville High School reviewed the guidelines that the districtwide planning group created at the Centerville School District character and conduct workshops the previous year. One part of the plan was to define and increase parent involvement on the basis of the character and conduct approach to improving student learning and safety. The planning group created a simple list for parent involvement that connected home and school roles and experiences. The table included the following elements:

- Developmental characteristics of the student
- Instructional strategies that help students develop the skills and knowledge they need to learn and stay safe
- Standards for learning and assessment
- Character and conduct standards and practices that home, school, and community share

The acronym DISC is a way to remember the ideas proposed by the group. Mr. Bracken, the athletic director, met with a subcommittee of the task force on athletics to consider strategies and activities for using the DISC approach to plan, implement, and evaluate practices in the athletic and physical education programs. The task force had three additional goals:

- To align the athletic program practices with the schoolwide curriculum, counseling, and discipline programs
- To incorporate the character and conduct approach into the athletic and physical education program
- To demonstrate the guiding principles of respect, impulse control, compassion, and equity within and beyond the athletic program

Input from Student Athletes

As Coach Noel led the procession of senior football players and their families across the playing field, he reflected how his feelings had changed in the year since the Centerville High School athletic program adopted the districtwide character and conduct initiative. As a 20-year veteran teacher, he had participated in professional development activities organized to demonstrate how all instructional staff can help students learn and stay safe. He was still surprised that the district had convened a task force on athletics to help student athletes develop team character standards and to transfer those standards to everyday life within and beyond the school. As a member of the task force, Coach Noel had been hesitant to change a winning athletic program that had brought pride to the district for years. After just two meetings, he began to question some of his own coaching methods, especially after a presentation by former student athletes and their parents.

During a presentation, one former athlete related an incident that left an indelible impression. The young man and two of his teammates had sat on the bench for most of the season. At one basketball game, the coach discussed the game plan during half-time and never used their names as part of any strategy. He called first-string players by name and referred to the second string as "the others." The coach didn't even look in their direction. The student was never sure that the coach knew his name or that he existed beyond the role of seldom-used backup for a star. Although this athlete was first string in another sport and went on to win an academic and athletic scholarship to college, this coach's action made him feel invisible and devalued. Although he had suffered no apparent long-term effects from that treatment, this former student wanted the task force to understand that such behavior could have devastating effects on the entire team and could create animosity between the starters and the second-string players.

He also explained how this coach's behavior sensitized him to the struggle faced by second-string athletes on the football team, on which he was a starting player. He saw how difficult it was for the second-string players to listen to the put-downs and heckling from their own classmates, who sometimes shouted that the second string had the best seat in the house to watch the game. He understood that the second-string players felt self-conscious about having clean uniforms as the starters left the field covered with mud—and pride.

Other former student athletes told how their parents quizzed them about why the coach didn't give them more playing time and accused them of not trying hard enough. Another former athlete shared how some members of the school staff would focus on the "stats" of the starting athletes or the team, whereas others seemed uninterested in athletic activities. All the athletes reported feeling some conflict between meeting the expectations on the field and in the classroom. As Coach Noel listened to each speaker, he began to see opportunities to integrate character and conduct standards into his coaching practices and into the entire school's approach to the athletic program (see Figure 5.1). He designed a parent participation workshop called Your Teen and Athletics. He required the parents of students who wanted to participate in the athletic program to attend the workshop to better understand

- The parent's role in the athletic program
- The student athlete's role
- The school's purpose in connecting learning, athleticism, sportsmanship, character, and conduct
- Ways for parents to make the character and conduct connection at home, at school, during games, and in the community

As Coach Noel returned to the bench and watched the last of the parents complete their walk with their senior student athletes and

---

Figure 5.1—Using DISC with the Athletic Program

The athletic department's workshop, Your Teen and Athletics, was designed for the parents of all students who want to participate in school sports. The workshop communicates the school's intention of helping students connect learning, athleticism, sportsmanship, character, and conduct to the games and to the students' behavior in the community. The workshop uses the principles of DISC to meet the goals.

The workshop addresses the **developmental characteristics of students** as it
• Meets student needs to connect with their parents through positive student interests.
• Helps parents understand how to support the physical, emotional, and intellectual health of their teens, with special emphasis on healthful lifestyles, nutrition, and stress management.
• Helps the students balance their roles as individuals and as members of a team representing the school and community.

The workshop has **instructional strategies** in place to
• Help parents understand how the coaches have incorporated the guiding principles into their coaching strategies and overall athletic program and how parents can use similar strategies to incorporate the character and conduct standards at home.

The workshop addresses **standards and assessments that students must meet or exceed** because it is
• Aligned with learning standards for health, National Collegiate Athletic Association (NCAA) standards for athletes, other federal and state guidelines, and local eligibility criteria.

The workshop encourages use of the **character and conduct approach** as it
• Engages students, teachers, and parents in applying respect, impulse control, compassion, and equity. For example, the workshop helps members of the school community identify and succeed within their respective roles; includes parents and educators; and celebrates the participation of all students.

---

take their places in the stands, he was proud of this new tradition at Centerville High School. Senior Day represented how the character and conduct approach had created clear connections among the student athletes, their families, and the school community as a whole. Coach Noel saw that the spectators understood their role as they cheered each senior whose name was called to take a place on the field. Although they did not see the usual first-string lineup, the crowd and the other players acknowledged and appreciated this starting team. As the game began, Assistant Coach Fine commented, "Hey, Coach, Senior Day was a good idea. I never saw those kids look so happy!"

The Coach's Plan

Until this year, starting quarterback Jerry Banks would never have believed that he would be happy to sit out the beginning of any game, much less the final home game of the season. Yet here he was, starting the game on the bench and rooting for his teammates, just the way they had rooted for him throughout the season. Being a part of the team felt different this year. From the first team meeting before the season began, Coach was doing and saying things differently than last year. Jerry had expected to walk into the first team meeting to talk about plays that work, winning attitudes, and getting in shape fast. This year, the first meeting was in a classroom and Coach asked the team members to think about what they wanted to learn from their experience as student athletes. Jerry had never given the question any thought. He just wanted to play. He had never thought about what he wanted to learn from playing and what the team might need from him beyond winning plays. That was the first day Coach started pushing the team theme—Competition and Cooperation with RICE!

Jerry had been learning about using RICE in the classroom and throughout the school, but he had not connected it with helping him and the team on the field. Jerry didn't know that his parents would be required to attend a workshop before he would be allowed to play a school sport. Through all of the small components, Jerry started to make connections about RICE with his coach, his parents, his teammates, and even his teachers. Jerry also began to understand that his primary goals were to learn and to stay safe and that the athletic program would support those goals.

This was the first year since he joined organized sports that Jerry felt that he could balance sports with other activities at school and in the rest of his life. Jerry used RICE-based game strategies to make everyday decisions and to solve ordinary problems. In the process, he began to appreciate the difference between winning and doing his best and developed some insight into his weaknesses. It was hard for Jerry to admit even one weakness, but now he was getting used to the idea that he did not have to be perfect or to win all the time. Of course, Jerry would play hard and do all he could to help his team win, but he also understood the importance of pregame preparation and frustration control when he got sacked. Although Jerry believed that there was no limit to what he could do, he could accept losing as part of the game and part of life. With the coach's guidance and his parents' support, Jerry began to apply respect, impulse control, compassion, and equity to sports.

Jerry's first chance to apply the guiding principles to sports happened when he injured an ankle during the second game of the season. As every time before when he'd been hurt, Jerry told the coach that he was well enough to play with his ankle heavily taped. Coach Noel's reminder to use the character and conduct connection left Jerry with only one option: sit out the game, let someone else play, and let his ankle heal. Jerry consciously used RICE to make a short-term decision for a long-term reason: He didn't want to lose the chance for a college scholarship or to injure himself permanently for just one game. After the game, Jerry discussed his decision with his parents. They told Jerry that they were proud of him for making the right decision for the right reason. His math teacher said exactly the same thing the next day.

As he watched the kickoff for the last home game of the season and the last regular season game of his high school career, Jerry reflected on how much more he had enjoyed playing football this year than any previous season.

Athletics as Part of the Curriculum, Counseling, and Discipline Programs

Right before kickoff, Ms. Barett looked around and noticed more school staff members at this game than had usually attended athletic events. She attributed increased attendance to the connectedness that the whole school felt to the athletic program and the athletes. The connections developed because the Centerville High School task force on athletics found opportunities to integrate the athletic program into the schoolwide program to promote learning and safety, and the athletic program integrated the character and conduct approach into its practices and procedures.

As the administrative representative on the task force, Ms. Barett recalled how the group set and made progress toward achieving three goals. To support the athletic program as part of the schoolwide curriculum, the task force promoted these activities:

• Encouraging a standard of practice that supports the entire instructional program (e.g., standards of conduct on the field are the same as in the hallways and classrooms for students, teachers, and coaches)

• Involving all faculty in departmental, grade-level, and faculty meetings in a variety of workshops on the guiding principles, even during seasons when faculty also have coaching responsibilities

• Rotating pep rallies and other noninstructional events during the school day so that no single class or period is interrupted regularly

  • Recognizing all teams by scheduling pep rallies in each season

  • Ensuring equity for all teams in terms of available resources

  • Encouraging faculty and staff to attend games

To identify and implement uniform safety and discipline procedures, the task force offered these suggestions:

• Ensuring equity in disciplinary action for all students regardless of their affiliation with a team or their role on a team

• Training all security in the Centerville High School Safe Schools Plan, which incorporates the character and conduct approach and includes special strategies for sports events, such as crowd control, entrance and egress routes and procedures, and safety drills

• Equipping security with easily recognizable jackets

• Conducting professional development activities so that all faculty and staff learn and follow the Safe Schools Plan in all circumstances

The task force also suggested ways to create opportunities for teachers to connect content areas to athletics and to include current topics, such as sports marketing for the general population:

• Incorporating team and sports concepts into the curriculum, such as sports journalism; the history of sports; statistics for teams and players; studying velocity, physiology, sports medicine, and other math- and science-related connections; sports in cultures outside the United States; and graphic arts illustrating sports and athleticism.

• Incorporating team and sports concepts into the discipline and counseling program by, for example, approaching formal education as a team activity and by exploring careers in sports—on and off the field

During this last game of the regular season, Ms. Barett felt confident that the Centerville High School athletic program was making progress toward achieving its goals and was proud of the role that she had played on that task force.

Figure 5.2 suggests how coaches and spectators can demonstrate respect, impulse control, compassion, and equity on and off the athletic field.

Figure 5.2—RICE and Tips Related to Athletes and Events

Coaches demonstrate RICE by modeling and directly teaching athletes to
- Respect themselves and show that self-respect in the way they treat others.
- Respect the game. Respect what they can learn from teamwork to succeed in the game and in life.
- Use impulse control.
- Use compassion toward themselves, their teammates, and any opponents.
- Use equity consistently.
- Use RICE to represent the school, team, and community.
- Win with class; lose with dignity.
- Work with the school community and model RICE-directed behavior.
- Schedule time to help parents demonstrate RICE at home as well as on the field.
- Meet with parents in workshops to discuss proper nutrition, fitness, and healthy lifestyles for student athletes.
- Work toward being a role model, a nurturer, a counselor, and a motivator to help student athletes get into college, get on a team, get into the world of work, and use RICE to manage conflict.
- Create press releases that celebrate a combination of winning, leadership, and team spirit.
- Be available for student athletes.
- Appreciate that each athlete is a student first.
- Adopt a theme, such as "Teamwork isn't everything, it's the only thing!"
- Establish that parents, spectators, and other members of the school community are part of the team.

Parents demonstrate and support RICE by
- Using appropriate language, cheering appropriately, following all school rules and laws regarding safety and security, and presenting a demeanor that encourages the athletes.
- Assisting students in getting picked up and dropped off on time, helping student athletes minimize and manage competing pressures, and talking with their athlete about what the child wants the parents to do as spectators. Parents should also be supportive by following procedures and seeing the game as an extension of the academic program. They can support the coach by allowing their child to follow the coach's game plan and by demonstrating impulse control, especially in helping their child debrief after the game. Parents should communicate with appropriate staff about physical, academic, or emotional issues faced by their child. Most important, parents should be available for their child and for the team.

Spectators, including student spectators, should
- Show RICE toward all athletes on all teams, practice good sportsmanship as a spectator, and follow all school rules and procedures.
- Be available for the team and team members.

6

Shoulder-to-Shoulder with Parents

Darlene Dowd couldn't believe that Ryan was starting kindergarten at Centerville Elementary School. Memories of first smiles, first coos, first words, first steps came flooding back and brought her near tears. Then she remembered 2 a.m. feedings, diaper rash, toilet training, and the terrible two's, followed by the hugs and goodnight kisses that still round out Ryan's day. It seemed as if he had just been born and as if he had been in her life forever. It was time for him to enter kindergarten. She just didn't know whether she was ready.

Although Darlene didn't feel quite ready for Ryan to begin kindergarten, she felt more prepared than she had a few years ago when his sister, Stacy, entered kindergarten. That was before the Centerville Elementary School adopted guiding principles to help students learn and stay safe.

All the members of the school, including the students, use guiding principles to define and fulfill their respective roles within the school setting. Parents and children use guiding principles to make positive connections between character and conduct at home and at school. Because parents help define the nature of their involvement at school, their understanding leads them to use similar strategies to create a home-based culture that supports learning within their own family traditions. This positive link creates continuity between students' home life and school life, thereby encouraging students to make the right decisions for the right reasons.

Students and their families experience key academic and developmental transitions from elementary through high school. Because transitions typically involve change, conflict, and adjustment, they offer excellent opportunities to strengthen the connection between school and home. All families can help students make successful transitions, even if the family's culture is significantly different from the school's culture. Families and schools can share many or few characteristics and still support student learning and safety. The way a student makes key school transitions can predict the way he will manage school, career, and personal transitions. Parents, educators, and students can use strategies based on guiding principles to help students make long-term and short-term decisions for long-term success.

Beginning Kindergarten

When Darlene and Tony Dowd received a letter about Ryan's appointment for kindergarten screening, they were surprised to see a festive card addressed to Ryan, inviting him to join other incoming kindergarten students to meet with the school nurse and some of the support staff at his new elementary school. The envelope also contained a copy of the Centerville Elementary School's *Chronicle* describing the guiding principles adopted by the Centerville School District. This newsletter included a Frequently Asked Questions section explaining what the guiding principles of respect, impulse control, compassion, and equity look and sound like at school and at home.

The Dowds also received a welcome letter from the principal and PTA president featuring important numbers, e-mail addresses, and Web sites for school-related information. The letter invited them to visit the special programs within the Centerville Elementary School Parent Resource Center during the kindergarten screening activities. To help students and families through the transition to kindergarten, the letter offered tips from parents, such as "Consider your hopes for your child. What do you hope for your child this year? In the future? Now consider one way you can use RICE today to help your child fulfill that dream. Discuss these hopes with your child and with the rest of your family. Consider how your everyday actions foster your child's short-term and long-term success."

The Dowds were surprised by the contents of the packet because it was different from the simple appointment letter they had received for Stacy's kindergarten screening. The information prompted Darlene and Tony to examine what they wanted and feared for their children and led them into a series of rewarding discussions that helped them discover important similarities and surprising differences.

For example, Darlene and Tony agreed that they hoped that their children would have strong family ties and would learn well in school. They feared that their children would be hurt or have difficulty in school. After thinking about a recent trip to the local mall, they realized that they had missed an opportunity to help their children connect with them and with each other. As Darlene and Tony reviewed this ordinary outing, they recognized how little interaction had taken place among family members. In the car, Tony and Darlene had listened to a CD, Stacy had set her headphones to a different CD, and Ryan had played a video game. They realized that this outing was typical of the way they spent their time as a family. Even though they were together in the car and in the mall, they were not interacting.

Darlene and Tony decided to use such everyday opportunities as car trips to listen to and speak with their children and with each other. Through daily conversation, they expected to get to know one another better and to help their children develop character and conduct that reflect the guiding principles promoted by the school and supported in their family. This was the first time that a letter from school had such a profound and positive effect on their thoughts and actions.

When the Dowds arrived at the school for the screening appointment, a parent welcomed them and directed them to the screening area, which was brightly decorated with balloons, posters celebrating RICE, and pictures of students engaged in school activities. They immediately noticed a picture of a program that included their daughter, Stacy.

For Darlene, the kindergarten screening reflected the new tone of the building, and she felt optimistic about her involvement as a parent. The optimism of the entire family grew stronger as they received additional letters of welcome and information. By the first day of school, Darlene, Tony, Stacy, and Ryan felt prepared for the opening days.

As Ryan walked into Centerville Elementary School, the teachers and administrators followed their plans to greet the children and escort them to class. Ryan recognized his teacher, Mr. Sheridan, from the picture he had enclosed in the "Welcome to Kindergarten" letter that Ryan had received during the summer. Mr. Sheridan followed his "first 10 days" plan to help Ryan and his classmates learn the purpose of school, get to know their classmates and schoolmates, and understand their own important role as active and valued members of their class and school.

Along with the rest of his classmates, Ryan began to learn how to use RICE. He illustrated examples of RICE by making drawings and telling stories. And, through role-play activities, Ryan learned that it is important for students to speak and that it is important for students to wait their turn to speak. In addition, the students drew pictures illustrating how they show respect by speaking and by waiting their turn at school. For homework, they brought their pictures home, explained to their parents how students show respect in school, and drew a picture illustrating what respect looks like at home. Mr. Sheridan's note to parents explained the concept of RICE and gave simple directions for the homework assignment. Alternative activities were made available, depending on the developmental readiness of the child.

Throughout the first 10 days, Mr. Sheridan gave the students a variety of structured opportunities to help them practice the guiding principles at school and at home. In his ongoing communication with parents, Mr. Sheridan shared tips to help parents incorporate RICE and daily homework routines into their family activities:

• Help your child use RICE to understand that important transitions, such as beginning kindergarten, are exciting, challenging, and rewarding.

• Reinforce how following routines can help everyone make transitions successfully.

• Develop a special homework routine that includes listening to your child explain the assignment; helping your child follow the teacher's directions to complete the activity; and encouraging your child to share accomplishments and feelings about school, classmates, homework, and other issues. Consider homework time an opportunity to connect with your child about his feelings and experiences.

• Initiate contact with your child's teacher and other appropriate school staff members to share information, to get answers to your questions, and to make a positive link between home and school.

• Help your child use RICE to organize homework and school-related tasks.

• Reach out to other parents through the Parent Resource Center and the Parent Teacher Association.

Ryan's first days of kindergarten prepared him for a successful transition into his role as a student in Centerville Elementary School. His transition was further supported when his parents participated in Back-to-School Night. Principal Griffin welcomed Darlene, Tony, and the other parents into the large-group activity room. She announced that the evening would begin with a short presentation by a panel of parents who were members of the Parent Resource Center. The panel members shared their perspectives on how parents can help their children make successful transitions. They defined the role of the parent as a partner working shoulder-to-shoulder with school staff to help children learn and stay safe, and they identified similarities and differences in the role of the student in the school and classroom and in the role of the child in the home and community.

After the whole-group presentation, Mr. Sheridan welcomed Darlene, Tony, and the other parents into the kindergarten class. The parents especially enjoyed seeing the children's work displayed throughout the class. The Dowds recognized the projects they had helped Ryan complete and viewed a five-minute slide show depicting how their children were learning to use RICE to learn and stay safe throughout each day in kindergarten. Throughout Mr. Sheridan's presentation, he emphasized that RICE was part of the existing curriculum, counseling, and discipline practices in all grade levels at Centerville Elementary School.

After Mr. Sheridan described key aspects of the kindergarten curriculum, he concluded the evening with a review of practical, specific parent tips to support learning and safety through the first few months of kindergarten. As Darlene and Tony left Back-to-School Night, they agreed that Mr. Sheridan had made some suggestions they could use to help Stacy make a successful transition into 4th grade.

Conferences with Parents

To prepare for the conferences with the 4th grade parents this year, Ms. Berger reviewed the guidelines that her districtwide planning group created at the Centerville School District Character and Conduct workshops in the previous year. These were the same guidelines that the athletic department had used to redefine the physical education program:

- Developmental characteristics of the student
- Instructional strategies that help students develop the skills and knowledge they need to learn and stay safe
- Standards for learning and assessment
- Character and conduct standards and practices that home, school, and community share

These guidelines (DISC) were the basis for two types of parent involvement strategies: strategies that schools can use to increase parent involvement (Figure 6.1) and strategies that parents can use to make connections between home and school (Figure 6.2).

Ms. Berger wanted to ensure that her parent-teacher conferences met the criteria of DISC, so she planned each meeting to include practical tips that parents could use to help their children transfer important skills from school to home. Just as she placed Stacy Dowd's portfolio on the desk for her parents to review, Darlene and Tony walked into the classroom and noticed that the room was decorated with posters illustrating what RICE looks like and sounds like at school and at home. Darlene and Tony quickly focused on Stacy's work and recognized some of the projects she had completed at home. In her letter to arrange their appointment, Ms. Berger had

Figure 6.1—Increasing Parent Involvement

The Centerville schools use parent-teacher conferences as an opportunity to use DISC strategies and to increase parent involvement in the school. Here's how the strategies align with parent-teacher conferences:

Developmental characteristics of students
- Students get positive recognition from parents and teachers as they focus on celebrating achievements.
- Students participate in personal growth and achievement as their teachers post grades and offer positive reinforcement. Students participate in celebrating their achievement as they explain their work to parents and receive positive reinforcement.

Instructional strategies
- Students are involved in independent and cooperative learning strategies as they prepare classwork, invitations, and the classroom for the conferences.

Standards and assessments
- Teachers align instruction with standards for English language arts (writing the invitation); art (designing the invitation and displays); and technology (using the computer to do some of the work and displays).

Character and conduct approach
- The preparation for and the actual conference engages students, teachers, and parents in applying respect, compassion, and equity. For example, the conference allows members of the school community to be identified and succeed within their roles; parents and teachers determine the best times for appointments; everyone celebrates the combined and individual achievement of all students.

invited Darlene and Tony to share concerns and ask questions. As Ms. Berger guided them through Stacy's portfolio and described her academic and social development in 4th grade thus far, Darlene and Tony raised related questions and shared observations. The topics they specifically covered included

- Preparing Stacy for state assessments and how her role as a learner gives her positive recognition for progress
- Supplying encouragement by having her parents stay involved in her assignments

---

Figure 6.2—School-to-Home Connections

Centerville schools use a check-in routine that addresses the conflicting needs and wants of students for independence and the needs and wants of the school and parents for student safety. The strategy is as useful at home as at school and can strengthen the connection students feel between home and school.

As part of the school curriculum, all students learn personal safety techniques, such as abduction prevention. A safety technique that students are taught is to always "check in" with the leader of the group and other group members before moving from one location to the next. For example, during recess a student wants a drink of water and checks in with the adult in charge before leaving the location.

At home this process takes places when a family member wants to leave the house. That family member checks in with the "adult in charge" and others to make sure the decision is appropriate at the time. Adults in the family also check in with other family members so everyone stays in touch. The check-in strategy fits the DISC principles:

Developmental characteristics of students
- Helps students fulfill their role as family members; fosters communication within the family; connects school-family practices.

Instructional strategies
- Builds on communication and collaboration techniques including shared and individual responsibility.

Standards and assessments
- Practice is aligned with health (personal safety and child abduction prevention), English language arts (communication), and social studies (student has a role to play in personal safety).

Character and conduct
- Engages students and parents in applying their roles, respect, impulse control, compassion, and equity. For example, it helps parents and students identify and succeed within their respective roles; involves family members in applying knowledge and skills developed in school; helps students actively participate in their own learning and safety.

- Emphasizing the use of stress management tips for balancing homework, study, and other activities

- Focusing on the guiding principles to promote a safe school environment

At the end of the conference, which was Ms. Berger's last one for the evening, she walked with them toward the main office, where Mrs. Griffin greeted them. After the Dowds said goodnight, the teacher and the principal shared some of their impressions about the evening. The next day, Ms. Berger gave Mrs. Griffin her completed conference feedback sheet, which identified trends in the questions that parents raised during the conferences. The feedback will help the principal plan the upcoming DISC workshops for parents.

One major trend that emerged from the conference feedback sheets at every grade level was parental concern about how to help children make the right decisions. Because educators shared this concern, the districtwide Parent Task Force agreed to have the first DISC workshop at each school concentrate on this theme. At the Centerville Middle School, this topic was timely, because middle-level students can be especially vulnerable to peers, media, and other influences that do not share the same standards of character and conduct promoted at school and at home.

Parent Workshops

When Robby Greene's mother attended a DISC workshop on helping middle school students make the right decisions, the first thing she saw was a mural in the front lobby proclaiming, "We Use RICE to Make the Right Decisions for the Right Reasons: Parents, Students, Children, and Educators Together." The theme was echoed throughout the school, on posters created by the students, and in the packet of materials that parents received. Sandy Greene was surprised to see how many parents had come to the workshop. She thought that only a few parents would be so concerned about decision making. As a single parent, Sandy Greene felt considerable pressure about making decisions. The members of the districtwide Parent Task Force, the planning committee, and the panel presenters were equally pleased at the large turnout and felt rewarded for choosing such a timely topic.

The workshop opened with a greeting from the middle school principal, Mr. Rutledge, who quickly reviewed the contents of the attendee packets. Each parent received a copy of the goal for the workshop: "Each of us will share and learn at least one way that parents and educators can help middle school children make the right decisions for the right reasons so that all our children learn and stay safe." The packet also contained a definition of the character and conduct approach, including RICE, and a definition of parent involvement for middle school students. Parents were reminded that they should know the purpose, members, roles, guiding principles, and procedures of the school; use RICE to communicate with their child and school personnel; and incorporate school-related learning goals, including RICE, into the family culture.

Examples of real-life situations showed how parents, middle school children, and educators can use the DISC format to help students make the right decisions for the right reasons under difficult circumstances. The packets included blank DISC charts for participants to complete during small-group activities and an evaluation form.

The PTA president led the participants through the agenda, which included agreements that participants and presenters would demonstrate RICE throughout the workshop; procedures for everyone to follow; and an outline of the sequence of events. The workshop began with the panel presentation, moved to the question-and-answer time and subsequent small-group activities led by facilitators, and culminated with closing activities and an announcement of the next workshop.

Throughout the program, the continuing yet changing importance of the parents' role was an ongoing theme. Parents and educators brainstormed strategies they could use to support the decision-making process of middle school students. The examples of decision areas facing middle school students and their parents ranged from appropriate clothing and haircuts to homework, dating, drug use, and violence.

The panelists led the participants through an activity to help them understand that students and adults who consistently apply the principles of RICE at home, at school, and in the community have additional resources for making the right decisions for the right reasons. For example, a student might consider how to use respect and impulse control to complete homework, visit with friends, or talk with her parents. A student would not cheat to do well on an exam or use a weapon to solve a problem, because the student had come to understand RICE. In addition, a student would be more likely to demonstrate RICE if her parents modeled the same guiding principles.

An important point that came out of the workshop was that "small stuff" to adults can really be "big stuff" to middle school students. All the participants agreed that using RICE to cope with the small stuff could help everyone apply the same guiding principles to the big stuff. For example, a parent member of the panel, Mr. Stanyo, related his own experience with defining and dealing with "stuff" with his middle school child. The issue was the television in his son's room.

> As soon as my wife and I installed the television in his room, it was as if he disappeared from the family. He watched TV alone in his room and basically stopped interacting with us. Now all of us can appreciate that we might welcome a short break from our middle school children, but this was not a short break. This was a loss, and we were distraught. We were also angry at ourselves for allowing it to happen. Our son did not respond to our repeated requests to come out of his room and join us in a variety of family activities. So my wife and I used RICE to bring our son back into our everyday family life. As we sat at dinner, we explained that we

missed the contact we had as family members. Because he had continued to isolate himself from the family in spite of our requests that he join us, we had decided to use the same approach we used with homework: There would be certain hours when he could be in his room alone, and others when he had to join us as a family member. We understood that the issue was not the television. The issue was keeping family connections, especially during the middle school years. We also understood that we had to make the time with us worthwhile—family discussions, games, even watching a TV program together and discussing it.

Ms. Ramirez, another member of the panel, concurred with Mr. Stanyo and discussed a similar issue. Her daughter was spending time in her room, talking on the telephone instead of connecting with the family. Others supported the point, noting how anything from television to the Internet to organized sports could distract parents from the core issue of the importance of making positive connections with children, even during difficult developmental stages. They shared how their approach to school involvement could actually strengthen their connections with their children.

In the small-group activities, parents used the DISC format to consider how to create opportunities for students to use RICE to achieve academic and personal goals. They defined media to include television, print, Internet, movies, radio, CDs, and video games. Although the members of the group disagreed on many media-related issues, they agreed to concentrate on one key point: helping middle-level students make the right decisions for the right reasons so that they can learn and stay safe.

As illustrated in Figure 6.3, Sandy Greene's group used the DISC format to consider how parents could be involved in their children's education by managing the role of media in their family life. For example, a 4th grader watches national TV and sees an elementary school student being arrested for shooting another elementary school student. Because the 4th grader is just beginning to sort

---

Figure 6.3—DISC and Media Strategies

Parents and teachers can guide students into making decisions about the appropriate use of media. For example, media can be used as a focal point of discussions.

Developmental characteristics of students
- Meets middle school students' powerful needs to establish their own identity, redefine relationships with parents, and create relationships with peers

Instructional strategies
- Matches schoolwide practices for cooperative learning, peer-assisted activities, and self-assessment

Standards and assessments
- Aligns with standards for health, English language arts, social studies, home and career, technology, and mathematics

Character and conduct approach
- Engages students and parents in defining appropriate roles and applying respect, impulse control, compassion, and equity

---

out his immediate reality and the reality of the world at large, his parents need to be involved in his media viewing habits so that they may consider the developmental character of the child and address the child's reactions to witnessing the event.

During the workshop, other parents echoed the concerns expressed by Sandy Greene. High school and elementary school parent representatives of the districtwide Parent Task Force who were attending the middle school workshop shared the same concerns about helping children make the right decisions for the right reasons. They explained that they were present to demonstrate their support for parents helping parents make connections from grade to grade and from home to school. They committed to sharing the middle-level parent concerns about decision making in general and media in particular when they reported back to their elementary and high school planning committees. This communication process resulted in a Centerville High School parent workshop with a similar theme.

Parents and the Driver Education Program

As they took their seats in the high school cafeteria, parents Bob DelRoy and Janet Young confided in each other that neither had attended a parent program since their children began middle school. They were surprised that they were required to attend this workshop for their children to be eligible for a school-sponsored driver's education program and to secure the privilege of a parking permit.

"I don't see the purpose of attending this program," Bob commented. "I see it as my son's responsibility to follow the rules and earn the privileges. I already know how to drive!" Janet laughed and agreed as the program began. The high school PTA president, Sarina Fox, opened the program by introducing the first speaker of the evening: Scott Wright, a graduate of Centerville High School, who related how his life had changed in a split second.

The audience fell silent as Scott told how the car he was driving suddenly swerved out of control when he was distracted by a conversation with his passengers. One of his friends was permanently injured; another friend suffered serious injuries. Scott explained that the accident could have happened to anybody, except for two things: Seven students were crowded into a car designed for five, and no one was wearing a seatbelt. He and the passengers had made a series of decisions that had long-term consequences beyond their imagination. Using the RICE approach to understanding decision making, Scott discussed how he and his friends did not demonstrate

- Respect for their own mortality or for the law requiring all drivers and passengers to wear seatbelts
- Impulse control when they crowded into the car instead of waiting for other transportation

• Compassion for their families, the members of their community, or for one another in the way they put themselves and others at risk

• Equity when they disregarded how their actions would unfairly burden their parents by causing undue stress and increased insurance liability

Scott's presentation focused the audience on just a few of parents' fears for their children. When Sarina Fox returned to the podium, she asked the parents to think about their best hopes for their teens as they worked in groups to manage their fears and articulate their hopes about "putting our teens in the driver's seat." Using the DISC format, Ms. Fox illustrated how their children would be involved as passengers or drivers in the coming years and explained how the content of the driver's education curriculum was connected to the standards set in the community and at home for driver etiquette, judgment, and responsibility (see Figure 6.4). She clarified that driving was a privilege, not a right, and that parking on school grounds was also a privilege that senior students could earn.

Ms. Fox encouraged the parents to use the remaining time to work in small groups and focus on four points related to students as drivers and passengers:

• Their best hopes for their children
• Their worst fears for their children
• Their role in helping their children use RICE to fulfill best hopes and avoid worst fears by making the right decisions for the right reasons
• Specific strategies that parents could use to help their children use school-based learning, school rules, public law, and family standards to stay safe by making the right decisions

Each group included a facilitator from the Centerville School District's pupil personnel department. Although the groups focused on different issues, common themes emerged regarding parents' roles:

• Model the driver behaviors and attitudes we want our children to use.
• Use impulse control to manage stress on the road.
• Attend driver education and safety courses with our children.
• Use RICE to establish procedures and conditions that govern our teenagers' automobile use, such deciding to drive sober and rested, not impaired by substances or fatigue.

The parents also learned strategies to keep their teenagers safe:

• Help teens use a check-in strategy (notifying a parent or identified adult) before taking the car from one location to another.
• Listen to teens express their priorities and concerns about driving.
• Talk with teens about the strategies we use to cope with our stress or anger as drivers.
• Ask our teens for their suggestions for coping with road rage, accidents, traffic jams, mechanical problems, and peer pressure to take driving risks.
• Be a regular passenger and observer as your teen drives; provide supportive, constructive, caring dialogue about driving and staying safe.

As Bob and Janet said goodnight to each other and to the other members of their group, they agreed that the night was more worthwhile than they had anticipated. They never thought that a school workshop would cause them to think so deeply about their roles as parents of teenage drivers. "I'm going to ask my son what he thinks about some of the things we talked about tonight. He wanted to pick up my daughter from the train station tonight. I think I'll ride with him as a passenger."

Figure 6.4—The Driving Curriculum

Learning to drive, that step teenagers typically take toward independence, is one example of how parents and educators can help students make the connection between school and home.

Parents hope teens will
✔ Drive safely
✔ Drive respectfully
✔ Follow laws, policies, and procedures on and off school campus
✔ Use RICE (friends help friends stay safe)

Learning to drive can be discussed using the DISC format:

Developmental characteristics: Driving offers teens developmentally appropriate possibilities including independence, peer support, an "identity," and parental approval.

Instructional strategies: Behind-the-wheel instruction gives teens practice in using cooperative learning activities, self-assessment, peer review, and problem-based learning.

Standards and assessments: Health, civics, math, science, and portfolios can be a part of the driving curriculum (e.g., each student portfolio contains techniques, such as using impulse control to set a limit on the number of kids in a car).

Character and conduct connections: Students use RICE in critical thinking and decision making to define their role as driver, passenger, or friend.

7

Getting Results

The students are ready to take their place in the moving-up procession at Centerville Middle School. Pat and the other 6th grade teachers join the ceremony to celebrate the accomplishments of students, faculty, and parents who made this event possible. As Pat watches the ceremonies unfold, she recognizes how using the guiding principles has transformed her own practices, her students, and even this moving-up ceremony. She observes how students, family members, and the rest of the audience demonstrate respect for the occasion and one another. Remembering previous moving-up ceremonies, including those of her own children, she recalls how students and members of the audience would talk during the ceremony, take photographs during times when they were asked to wait, and call out at inappropriate times. During this ceremony, the audience and the students conduct themselves with a sense of shared purpose and dignity.

After the festivities, Pat and her colleague Allen discuss the moving-up ceremonies as they walk to the parking lot. Pat observes, "Everyone's conduct was so much better this year." Allen laughs and says, "I have to admit that this year was different. Let's see what everyone else says at the professional development workshop next week."

A week later, Pat and Allen join the rest of their middle school team at the districtwide workshop. The agenda includes three discussion items regarding the character and conduct approach:

- Evaluating results in relation to goals
- Continuing to integrate technology into the instructional, counseling, discipline, and safety initiatives
- Using data to plan professional development activities

The teams agreed to divide patterns of student conduct and school practices into two domains: small stuff and big stuff. Examples of small stuff for student conduct and school practices included noise levels; hallway routines and cleanliness; punctuality; homework patterns; classroom climate; maintenance and repair routines; conduct on buses; and evidence of respect, impulse control, compassion, and equity. Examples of big stuff included patterns of cutting classes and bullying; dropout rates; attendance; in-school and out-of-school suspensions; fights; assaults; drug- or alcohol-related incidents; weapons; theft; vandalism; bombs; arson; any kind of bias incidents; harassment; and all other kinds of threatening behaviors.

The members of the Centerville school community posed the hypothesis: "If the Centerville school community uses RICE to address small, everyday acts in school, then the normative structure of the school will improve." As a result, they believed, the "big stuff" will reflect the shared purpose of the school, which is to help all students learn well and stay safe. Pat and Allen helped formulate this statement during the workshops a year ago and were motivated to work with their colleagues to examine any data that might support or challenge the hypothesis.

The Centerville school community integrated guiding principles into all its practices. In the process, students were taught how to make connections between what they learn in class and what they do on a day-to-day basis. The teaching, counseling, and discipline programs were designed to help students use RICE to consciously make the right decisions for the right reasons. Administrators, teachers, pupil personnel, support staff, and parents can build a strong sense of shared purpose that fosters cooperation, communication, and positive outcomes for students at Centerville.

All members of the Centerville school community—teachers and counselors, administrators and parents, other staff and students—make their schools learning communities. Through their shared and individual voices, Centerville shows how a school community can adapt the aspects of character appropriate for their school to promote and how it can use character education activities to achieve learning and safety goals.

Through the everyday experiences of the Centerville school community, these educators have demonstrated how they use a basic principle of teaching and learning that has sustained public education for generations: *Schools teach and measure what is important to the school and to the community.* This is as true for reading and math as it is for character and conduct. For example, every reading program includes instructional and evaluation components. The same is true for every other area, from mathematics to music. Educators can experience the same levels of success when they use a character and conduct approach that includes instructional and evaluation components.

We leave the Centerville staff as they begin to evaluate how consistently and correctly their practices reflect their intended approach to character and conduct. We devote the final parts of this chapter to recommending how educators can evaluate the success of the character and conduct approach in schools or in districts. Our recommendations focus on evaluating results in relation to learning and safety goals and using data to plan professional development activities. We chose these areas of concentration because the majority of districts, schools, and other organizations we have worked with have expressed interest in these areas.

It is our experience that schools and districts benefit from using qualitative (testimony from parents, teachers, students, and others in the school community) and quantitative data to plan and evaluate their own character and conduct approach to achieving learning and safety goals and to plan for professional development. Although many sources and strategies for collecting, interpreting, and reporting data are available, we have included several examples that schools and districts may complete easily as part of their existing evaluation routines.

Evaluating Learning and Safety Goals

Most educators already use both qualitative and quantitative data to plan, implement, and evaluate practices and programs. We recommend that educators incorporate a hypothesis into the planning process and test that hypothesis on the basis of evidence that all parties value, such as academic success and safety. We suggest that districts implementing guiding principles consider the following two hypotheses:

• If student conduct and school safety improve, then student learning will improve.
• If teaching, discipline, and counseling practices are aligned on the basis of the character and conduct approach, then student learning will improve.

In Figure 7.1, we list some of the data that schools may choose to collect. Depending on fiscal conditions or proximity to a cooperating university, some schools will have fairly modest ways to collect data; other schools will be more ambitious. We recommend that schools collect some baseline data related to that school's goals, and

Figure 7.1—Collecting and Measuring Data

Without collecting baseline data, it will be difficult to show actual results from adopting any kind of new strategy or curriculum. The following suggestions can help you get started, without overwhelming your staff or budget.

Type or Source of Data	Performance Indicators
Grades	• Increase mastery levels to 85 percent or higher.
Results of standardized and other normed assessments	• Increase percentage of students meeting or exceeding local and state norms.
Graduation rates	• Strive for 100 percent.
Promotion or retention patterns and gateways	• Establish patterns, set benchmarks, and meet or exceed goals.
Gains made in response to academic intervention services and other support strategies	• Identify needs and strengths. • Use best practices to match students to services.
Advanced Placement results	• Promote Advanced Placement course offerings. • Promote diversity of teachers and students in Advanced Placement classes. • Increase the number of students earning a score of 3 or better on Advanced Placement examinations.
Participation in National Merit, Honor Society, Honor Roll, and other organizations dedicated to excellence in academic and vocational areas of study	• Promote academic and vocational excellence initiatives. • Increase participation.
Longitudinal data to indicate number of students who complete two- or four-year colleges or other postsecondary educational experiences	• Create, implement, analyze, and use data from the Exit Survey of Graduating Seniors (Appendix D). • Create an alumni association.
Number of fights	• Reduce the frequency and severity of conflicts and fights.
Number of bus incidents	• Reduce referrals from bus drivers. • Reduce student and parent complaints.
Number of suspensions	• Reduce frequency of in-school suspension. • Reduce frequency of out-of-school suspensions.

at six-month intervals, collect data to see if they are on track. In the process of achieving learning and safety goals, results can occur incrementally. In our experience, a school or district can take from one to three years to transform its normative structure across all grade levels.

By using the categories of data described in Figure 7.1, schools and districts can track and achieve progress toward performance indicators through meaningful professional development activities. Although much of the data is quantifiable (rate of cutting classes, attendance, grades, test scores), do not underestimate the value of teacher, parent, and student surveys and testimony. Use that information in creating a professional development program to improve student learning and safety.

Professional Development

Educators report the most significant gains in student learning and school safety when the professional development program includes the characteristics described in Figure 7.2. Because guiding principles are designed to transform the normative structure of the school, participants in all the professional development programs use RICE to engage in their own learning and to align their curriculum, instruction, assessment, counseling, and discipline activities.

The form and variety of professional development activities can vary, depending on the goals, school or district culture, and financial resources. On-site workshops, action research, mentoring, online learning, and distance learning can work, although some on-site workshops and collegial sharing are required.

Professional development initiatives are likely to succeed when educators use data to evaluate programs, assess student needs, and plan professional development on the basis of student performance. Data-driven practices are particularly valuable when a school or district integrates the character and conduct approach into the teach-

Figure 7.2—Characteristics of Effective Professional Development	
Characteristic	**Description**
Related to board, district, and school goals	Builds capacity through budgetary practices
Based on data	Reflects current data on student learning and school safety
Job-embedded	Relates directly to teaching, counseling, and disciplinary practices focusing on student character- and conduct-related needs and strengths
Collaboratively designed	Includes members of educator groups responsible for teaching, counseling, and discipline practices in the design, implementation, and evaluation of professional development activities that incorporate the character and conduct approach
Continually assessed	Follows a schedule in which formative and summative data are gathered, analyzed, reviewed, reported, and used to change or sustain practices
Ongoing	Evolves continuously to sustain the use of effective practices reflecting the guiding principles of character and conduct

ing, discipline, and counseling practices. Data help all participants measure the progress they are making toward their goals.

Through tragic lessons that continue to grab headlines, our children have taught us that safety, learning, character, and conduct are inextricably connected. We do not have to stand at the edge of the grave of a child or adult cut down by school violence to know we must do what we do best right now: teach our children that we belong to each other, that we respect each other, that we connect with each other. Metal detectors and surveillance equipment will not keep us safe. The most important safety feature in a school is the welcoming, inclusive approach it takes to help all children learn what they need to know and do in our academic program, our hall-ways, and throughout our schools to achieve, to participate, to respect each other, to get help when they need it, and to feel secure.

We cannot protect our children from facing difficult questions. We can help them develop the character and conduct they need to answer those questions, so they make the right decisions for the right reasons. They depend on us to help them learn and stay safe. Their future—and ours—depends on how well we succeed.

Appendix A: Needs Assessment

This needs assessment becomes a job and strength analysis as every-one works together to close the gap between what students are doing and what they should be doing. It also helps everyone in the community celebrate what students are doing right.

Name: _____ Date: _____
                (Optional)

Current school: (Check all that apply)
____ Centerville ES   ____ Centerville MS
____ Centerville HS   ____ Centerville Central Office

Total years in education profession:
____ 0–5 years   ____ 6–10 years   ____ 11–15 years
____ 16–21 years   ____ 21+ years

Current job title or description:
____ Teacher
____ Administrator
____ Pupil Personnel
____ Classroom Support Staff (teacher aides, teacher assistants)
____ Noninstructional Support Staff (clerical, security, monitors, custodial)
____ Other (please specify): _____

Grade level: (check all that apply)
____ PreK ____ K–1 ____ 2–3 ____ 4–5 ____ MS ____ HS

Subjects: (check all that apply)

____ English	____ Social Studies	____ Math	____ Science
____ Health	____ Physical Ed.	____ Art	____ Music
____ Computer	____ Languages	____ ESL	____ Business
____ Reading	____ Technology	____ Home & Careers	
____ Special Ed.	____ Library	____ Speech	
____ Other (specify): _____			

Category of Concern	Always	Sometimes	Never	Not Sure
1.0 What are the students doing right now?				
1.1 Calling out	___	___	___	___
1.2 Interrupting one another	___	___	___	___
1.3 Speaking disrespectfully and impulsively	___	___	___	___
1.4 Listening to directions	___	___	___	___
1.5 Following directions	___	___	___	___
1.6 Completing assignments	___	___	___	___
1.7 Arriving at school on time	___	___	___	___
1.8 Arriving at class on time	___	___	___	___
1.9 Arriving prepared to learn and participate	___	___	___	___
1.10 Using appropriate language	___	___	___	___
1.11 Attending class	___	___	___	___
1.12 Demonstrating respect	___	___	___	___
1.13 Using positive interpersonal skills	___	___	___	___
1.14 Following classroom procedures	___	___	___	___
1.15 Following school procedures	___	___	___	___
1.16 Participating positively in class	___	___	___	___

	Always	*Sometimes*	*Never*	*Not Sure*
1.17 Fulfilling the role of the student in school	—	—	—	—
1.18 Connecting with at least one other adult in school	—	—	—	—
1.19 Handling frustration appropriately	—	—	—	—
1.20 Following safety procedures	—	—	—	—
1.21 Demonstrating compassion	—	—	—	—
1.22 Promoting equity	—	—	—	—
1.23 Expressing opinions about the future	—	—	—	—
1.24 Using decision-making skills appropriately	—	—	—	—
1.25 Providing positive peer support	—	—	—	—
1.26 Demonstrating understanding of the purpose of school	—	—	—	—
1.27 Demonstrating knowledge of who the members of the school community are	—	—	—	—

2.0 We have referenced the following sources of data regarding the student behaviors listed in the 1.0 series (above).

2.1 Incident reports	—	—	—	—
2.2 Discipline referrals	—	—	—	—
2.3 Suspensions	—	—	—	—
2.4 Detentions	—	—	—	—
2.5 Letters to parents or guardians regarding disciplinary issues	—	—	—	—
2.6 Letters to parents or guardians regarding academic issues	—	—	—	—

	Always	Sometimes	Never	Not Sure
2.7 Bus incidents	___	___	___	___
2.8 School report card data	___	___	___	___
2.9 Results of assessments	___	___	___	___
2.10 Honors-related data	___	___	___	___

3.0 What do we want students to demonstrate knowledge and mastery of?

	Always	Sometimes	Never	Not Sure
3.1 The purpose of school	___	___	___	___
3.2 The members of the school community	___	___	___	___
3.3 The roles of the members of the school community	___	___	___	___
3.4 The guiding principles and rules of the school	___	___	___	___
3.5 The procedures of the school	___	___	___	___
3.6 The procedures of the classroom	___	___	___	___
3.7* Controlling the impulse to speak out of turn	___	___	___	___
3.8 Listening to the end of the other person's sentence	___	___	___	___
3.9 Listening for understanding	___	___	___	___
3.10 Speaking respectfully so others understand	___	___	___	___
3.11 Following directions	___	___	___	___

4.0 What are our resources to close the gap between 1.0 and 3.0?

	Always	Sometimes	Never	Not Sure
4.1 Our instructional staff	___	___	___	___
4.2 Our pupil personnel	___	___	___	___

---

* Beginning with line 3.7, items reflect examples of what your school or district might choose to identify to work on. The items are related to the problems identified in Section 1.0.

		Always	Sometimes	Never	Not Sure
4.3	Our administrators	—	—	—	—
4.4	Our noninstructional staff	—	—	—	—
4.5	Our students	—	—	—	—
4.6	Our parent and community members	—	—	—	—
4.7	Our curriculum	—	—	—	—
4.8	Our discipline program	—	—	—	—
4.9	Our facilities	—	—	—	—
4.10	Our fiscal resources	—	—	—	—
5.0	**What obstacles might get in our way?**				
5.1	Inconsistent application of our guiding principles plan	—	—	—	—
5.2	Miscommunication among members of the school community	—	—	—	—
5.3	Lack of support from stakeholders	—	—	—	—
5.4	Insufficient resources applied to the guiding principles project	—	—	—	—
5.5	Inadequate or incorrect data used to develop or monitor the guiding principles project	—	—	—	—
6.0	**How will we monitor our progress?**				
6.1	Set benchmarks to close the gap between 1.0 and 3.0	—	—	—	—
6.2	Schedule periodic assessment of implementation and student learning	—	—	—	—
6.3	Modify implementation as needed	—	—	—	—

Appendix B: Assignments and Notes

The student handbook includes information about the purpose of the school, a list of the school members and their key roles as they relate to the students, excerpts of school policies, and the guiding principles and procedures that drive the school. In addition, the handbook includes the school calendar, a brief explanation of study skills, home-to-school communication guides, and space for students to record assignments, notes, and other important information. This excerpt represents the weekly format that focuses on assignments and notes. In each period, the student uses the handbook to record important points, such as an upcoming quiz in social studies or a report due in English. This format helps remind students to reflect on their assignments.

The following pages show an excerpt from the *Character and Conduct Student Handbook: High School Edition*. The student handbook is 5″ × 7″ so it is easy for students and staff to use, carry, and store.

September

Sunday 9/10	Monday 9/11	Tuesday 9/12	Wednesday 9/13	Thursday 9/14	Friday 9/15	Saturday 9/16
Focus	Focus	Focus	Focus	Focus	Focus	Focus
1	1	1	1	1	1	1
2	2	2	2	2	2	2
3	3	3	3	3	3	3
4	4	4	4	4	4	4
5	5	5	5	5	5	5
6	6	6	6	6	6	6
Reflect	Reflect	Reflect	Reflect	Reflect	Reflect	Reflect

RICE

R espect

I mpulse control

C ompassion

E quity

Make the right decisions for the right reasons!

Appendix C: Progress Report for Behavior Replacement Plan

Student: _____ Date: _____

Administrator or Initiator: _____

Teacher: _____

Subject or Class: _____ Period: _____

Goal 1: _____

_____

Goal 2: _____

_____

Goal 3: _____

_____

Date and actions that prompted the creation of the behavior replacement plan: _____

_____

_____

Since the date of the incident (or the most recent assessment):
1. The student demonstrates positive interpersonal skills in class.
   ☐ Always   ☐ Sometimes   ☐ Never

2. The student follows classroom procedures.
   ☐ Always   ☐ Sometimes   ☐ Never

3. Communication between home and school was initiated by
   ☐ School staff   ☐ Parent or guardian
   ☐ There hasn't been any communication

4. How is the student using RICE to achieve personal goals?

5. Since the incident or progress report on _____ (date), the student's attendance and work is recorded as follows.

	Date	Date	Date	Date	Date	Date
Absences						
Late Arrivals						
Cut Classes						

Passed _____ of _____ tests and quizzes.

Completed _____ of _____ homework and assignments.

_____   _____
Student's signature   Staff member's signature

Appendix D: Exit Survey of Graduating Seniors

This instrument is one of a series of surveys that staff can use to assess and improve services to all students and parents or guardians. High school seniors can offer staff valuable feedback about the degree to which school procedures meet four areas of student needs: scheduling; making connections with others; having opportunities to participate; and planning for life after high school. Other survey instruments can provide feedback from students who have already graduated and can evaluate how high school prepared them for postsecondary experiences, such as employment, college, and community life.

Directions: Please read each item carefully.
Please check <u>one</u> (1) answer for each item.
Thank you!

Example:

		Always	Sometimes	Never	Not Sure
0	The Grade Level Orientation Program was helpful to me each year.	__	✔	__	__

1.0 These items are about *scheduling*.

		Always	Sometimes	Never	Not Sure
1.1	Staff members helped me learn that a purpose of school is to learn well and stay safe.	__	__	__	__
1.2	Staff members helped me learn that my role as a student is to help myself and others learn well and stay safe.	__	__	__	__

		Always	Sometimes	Never	Not Sure
1.3	In school, I received good information about graduation requirements.	—	—	—	—
1.4	In school, I learned how to choose the right sequence of courses for me.	—	—	—	—
1.5	The course-offering handbook was <u>not</u> easy to use.	—	—	—	—
1.6	The course-offering handbook helped me make the right course selections.	—	—	—	—
1.7	My counselor helped me make the right course selections.	—	—	—	—
1.8	My counselor helped me use RICE to make decisions for the right reasons.	—	—	—	—
1.9	The class schedule I planned was <u>not</u> the schedule I received.	—	—	—	—
1.10	I did <u>not</u> understand the rules for changing my schedule.	—	—	—	—
1.11	The school staff followed the rules for changing students' schedules.	—	—	—	—
1.12	Before the first day of school, I changed my schedule.	—	—	—	—
1.13	In the first three weeks of school, I changed my schedule.	—	—	—	—
1.14	After the first three weeks of school, I changed my schedule.	—	—	—	—

	Always	Sometimes	Never	Not Sure

1.15 If I needed to change a course,
it was changed in more than
five school days.   —   —   —   —

1.16 In general, the scheduling and
course-selection services were
helpful.   —   —   —   —

2.0 These items are about making *connections with others*.

2.1 People in our school treat each
other with RICE (respect, impulse control, compassion, and
equity).   —   —   —   —

2.2 If I had a question, I got help
from at least one adult at school.   —   —   —   —

2.3 If I had a question, I could <u>not</u>
get help from another student.   —   —   —   —

2.4 There was at least one adult in
the school with whom I talked
on a regular basis.   —   —   —   —

2.5 There was at least one student
in the school with whom I
talked on a regular basis.   —   —   —   —

2.6 If I had a crisis, I would <u>not</u> go
to any adult in school.   —   —   —   —

2.7 If I had a crisis, there was at least
one student in school to whom
I would go.   —   —   —   —

2.8 In general, I felt that I could get
the help I needed at school.   —   —   —   —

	Always	Sometimes	Never	Not Sure

3.0 These items are about how your school gave you *opportunities to participate* in courses, clubs, sports, and other activities.

3.1 I did <u>not</u> have opportunities to develop my interests and abilities in class. — — — —

3.2 I did have out-of-class, school-related opportunities to develop my interests. — — — —

3.3 The guidance department helped me explore my interests and abilities. — — — —

3.4 I did participate in clubs and activities. — — — —

3.5 The coaches and advisors I worked with made the activities enjoyable. — — — —

3.6 The students I worked with did <u>not</u> demonstrate RICE. — — — —

3.7 In general, my school experience helped me develop my interests and abilities. — — — —

4.0 These items are about *planning for the years after high school*, including making the right decisions for the right reasons about college, career, and other important things.

4.1 The guidance department helped me discover education opportunities that I can use after high school.

		Always	Sometimes	Never	Not Sure
4.2	The guidance department helped me discover employment and career opportunities I can use after high school.	—	—	—	—
4.3	I was <u>not</u> given helpful information about when and how to participate in SATs, college application activities, and scholarships.	—	—	—	—
4.4	I was given helpful information about participating in employment fairs, job-shadowing programs, and other career-related opportunities.	—	—	—	—
4.5	In general, the school staff treated my dreams and goals with respect.	—	—	—	—
4.6	In general, the school staff helped me plan for my years after high school.	—	—	—	—

Appendix E: Staff Survey
of High School Services for Students

Please read each item carefully. Please check one answer for each item. Return the survey to the box in the front office labeled "Staff Survey."

Example:

                Always *Sometimes* *Never* *Not Sure*

0   The Grade Level Orientation
Program was helpful to me
each year.   —   ✔   —   —

1.0 These items are about *scheduling.*

1.1 Staff members helped students
learn that a purpose of school is
to learn well and stay safe.   — — — —

1.2 Staff members helped students
learn that the role of a student
is to help himself and others
learn well and stay safe.   — — — —

1.3 Students received good
information about graduation
requirements.   — — — —

1.4 Students learned how to
choose the right sequence of
courses for themselves.   — — — —

1.5 The course-offering handbook
was <u>not</u> easy for students to use. — — — —

	Always	Sometimes	Never	Not Sure
1.6 The course handbook helped students make the right course selections.	—	—	—	—
1.7 Counselors helped students make the right course selections.	—	—	—	—
1.8 Counselors helped students use RICE to make decisions for the right reasons.	—	—	—	—
1.9 The class schedules that students planned did not match the schedules that the students received.	—	—	—	—
1.10 Students did not understand the rules for changing their schedules.	—	—	—	—
1.11 The school staff followed the rules for changing students' schedules.	—	—	—	—
1.12 Before the first day of school, students changed their schedules.	—	—	—	—
1.13 In the first three weeks of school, students changed their schedules.	—	—	—	—
1.14 After the first three weeks of school, students changed their schedules.	—	—	—	—
1.15 If students needed to change a course, it took more than five school days to make the change.	—	—	—	—

Always   Sometimes   Never   Not Sure

1.16 In general, the scheduling and
      course-selection services were
      helpful.   —   —   —   —

2.0 These items are about making connections with others.

2.1   People in our school treat one
      another with RICE (respect,
      impulse control, compassion,
      and equity).   —   —   —   —

2.2   If students had a question, they
      got help from at least one adult
      at school.   —   —   —   —

2.3   If students had a question, they
      could <u>not</u> get help from another
      student.   —   —   —   —

2.4   There was at least one adult
      in the school with whom each
      student talked on a regular basis.   —   —   —   —

2.5   There was at least one student
      in the school with whom each
      student talked on a regular basis.   —   —   —   —

2.6   If a student had a crisis, he would
      <u>not</u> go to an adult in school.   —   —   —   —

2.7   If a student had a crisis, there
      was at least one student in
      school to whom he would go.   —   —   —   —

2.8   In general, students felt that
      they could get needed help
      in school.   —   —   —   —

Always   Sometimes   Never   Not Sure

3.0 **These items are about how your school gives students opportunities to participate in courses, clubs, sports, and other activities.**

3.1   Students did <u>not</u> have opportunities to develop their interests and abilities in class.   ___   ___   ___   ___

3.2   Students did have out-of-class, school-related opportunities to develop their interests.   ___   ___   ___   ___

3.3   The guidance department helped students explore their interests and abilities.   ___   ___   ___   ___

3.4   Students did participate in clubs and activities.   ___   ___   ___   ___

3.5   The coaches and advisors made the activities enjoyable for the students.   ___   ___   ___   ___

3.6   The students did <u>not</u> demonstrate RICE.   ___   ___   ___   ___

3.7   In general, our school experience helped students develop their interests and abilities.   ___   ___   ___   ___

4.0 **These items are about planning for the years after high school, including making the right decisions for the right reasons about college, career, and other important things.**

4.1   The guidance department helped students discover education opportunities they can use after high school.   ___   ___   ___   ___

Always   Sometimes   Never   Not Sure

4.2 The guidance department helped
students discover employment
and career opportunities they
can use after high school.   —   —   —   —

4.3 Students were <u>not</u> given helpful
information about when and
how to participate in SATs,
college-application
activities, and scholarships.   —   —   —   —

4.4 Students were given helpful
information about participating
in employment fairs, job-
shadowing programs, and
other career-related
opportunities.   —   —   —   —

4.5 In general, the school staff
treated students' dreams
and goals with respect.   —   —   —   —

4.6 In general, school staff helped
students plan for their years after
high school.   —   —   —   —

Resources

Achenbach, T., & Howell, C. (1993). Are American children's problems getting worse? A thirteen-year comparison. *Journal of the American Academy of Child and Adolescent Psychiatry, 32*, 1145–1154.

Amundson, K. (1991). *Teaching values and ethics: Problems and solutions.* Arlington, VA: American Association of School Administrators.

Anderson, J. (1990). *Cognitive psychology and its implications.* New York: W. H. Freeman.

Bennett, W. (1993). *The book of virtues.* New York: Simon & Schuster.

Binfet, J. T. (1995). Creating a positive moral climate within the public school classroom: An application of moral reasoning theory to practice. *Moral Education Forum, 20*(1), 18–24.

Bronfenbrenner, U. (1979). *The ecology of human development.* Cambridge, MA: Harvard University Press.

Brophy, J. E., & Alleman, J. (1991). Activities as instructional tools: A framework for analysis and evaluation. *Educational Researcher, 20*(4), 9–23.

Brown, D. F., & Varady, J. (1997, March). Re-examining the writing of Dr. Seuss to promote character development. *Middle School Journal,* 28–32.

Coles, R. (1989). *The call of stories: Teaching and the moral imagination.* Boston: Houghton-Mifflin.

Coles, R. (1990). *The spiritual life of children.* Boston: Houghton Mifflin.

Coles, R. (1997b). *The moral intelligence of children.* New York: Random House.

Coles, R., & Genevie, L. (1990). The moral life of America's school children. *Teacher, 1*(6), 43–49.

Cooperative Learning. (1989/1990, December/January). *Educational Leadership, 47*(4).

Curwin, R. L. (1995). A humane approach to reducing violence in schools. *Educational Leadership, 52*(5), 72–75.

Czikszentmihali, M. (1984). *Being adolescent: Conflict and growth in the teenage years.* New York: Basic Books.

Damon, W. (1985). *The moral child.* New York: Free Press.

Damon, W. (1993). Foreword. In A. Garrod (Ed.), *Approaches to moral development* (pp. ixx). New York: Teachers College Press.

Damon, W. (1995). *Greater expectations: Overcoming the culture of indulgence in our homes and schools.* New York: Free Press.

Darling-Hammond, L. (1994). *Professional development in schools: Schools for developing a profession.* New York: Teachers College Press.

Darling-Hammond, L., Wise, A. E., & Klein, S. P. (1999). *A license to teach: Raising standards for teaching.* San Francisco: Jossey-Bass.

Davidson, F. H., & Davidson, M. M. (1994). *Changing childhood prejudice: The caring work of schools.* Westport, CT: Bergin & Garvey.

Davis, G. (1993, March). Creative teaching of moral thinking: Fostering awareness and commitment. *Middle School Journal*, 32–33.

Eisenberg, N. (1992). *The caring child*. Cambridge, MA: Harvard University Press.

Ellenwood, S., & McLaren, N. (1994). Literature-based character education. *Middle School Journal*, 42–47.

Emler, E. (1996). How can we decide whether moral education works? *Journal of Moral Education, 25*(1), 117–126.

Emmer, E. T., Evertson, C. M., Clements, B. S., & Worsham, M. E. (1997). *Classroom management for secondary teachers* (4th ed.). Boston: Allyn & Bacon.

English, F. W. (1988). *Curriculum auditing*. Cincinnati, OH: Technomic.

Evertson, C. M., Emmer, E.T., Clements, B. S., & Worsham, M. E. (1997). *Classroom management for elementary teachers* (4th ed.). Boston: Allyn & Bacon.

Gardner, H. (1991). *To open minds*. New York: Basic Books.

Gardner, H. (1995). *Leading minds*. New York: Basic Books.

Gardner, H. (1999). *The disciplined mind: What all students should know and understand*. New York: Simon & Schuster.

Gilligan, C. (1982). *In a different voice*. Cambridge, MA: Harvard University Press.

Gilligan, C. (1990). *Mapping the moral domain*. Cambridge, MA: Harvard University Press.

Glasser, W. (1984). *Control theory*. New York: Harper & Row.

Goleman, D. (1995). *Emotional intelligence*. New York: Bantam.

Goodlad, J. I. (1984). *A place called school*. New York: McGraw-Hill.

Hawthorne, R. K. (1992). *Curriculum in the making: Teacher choice and the classroom experience*. New York: Teachers College Press.

Hoffman, M. (1991). Empathy, social cognition and moral action. In W. Kurtines & J. Gerwitz (Eds.), *Handbook of moral behavior and development* (Vol. 1, pp. 275–302). Hillsdale, NJ: Erlbaum.

Hope, W. C. (1997, March). Meeting the needs of middle level students through service learning. *Bulletin*, 39–45.

Jackson, P. W., Boostrom, R. E., & Hansen, D. T. (1998). *The moral life of schools*. San Francisco: Jossey-Bass.

Jacobs, H. H. (1997). *Mapping the big picture*. Alexandria, VA: ASCD.

Johnson, S. M. (1990). *Teachers at work*. New York: Basic Books.

Joseph, J. (1994). *The resilient child*. New York: Plenum Press.

Keeney, R. (1992). *Value-focused thinking: A path to creative decision-making*. Cambridge, MA: Harvard University Press.

Kohlberg, L. (1968). The child as a moral philosopher. *Psychology Today, 7*, 25–30.

Kohlberg, L. (1974). *The psychology of moral development*. New York: Harper.

Kohlberg, L. (1975). This special section in perspective. *Social Education*, 213–215.

Kohn, A. (1996). *Beyond discipline*. Alexandria, VA: ASCD.

Kohn, A. (1997, February). How not to teach values. *Phi Delta Kappan*, 429–439.

Konner, M. (1991). *Childhood: A multicultural view*. Boston: Little, Brown.

Kozol, J. (1991). *Savage inequalities*. New York: Harper Perennial.

Lawrence-Lightfoot, S. (1983). *The good high school: Portraits of character and culture*. New York: Basic Books.

Lawrence-Lightfoot, S. (1999). *Respect: An explanation*. Reading, MA: Perseus Books.

Marzano, R. J. (1992). *A different kind of classroom: Teaching with dimensions of learning*. Alexandria, VA: ASCD.

National School Boards Association. (1987). *Building character in the public schools*. Alexandria, VA: Author.

Piaget, J. (1965). *The moral judgment of the child*. New York: Free Press.

Ramsey, C. A. (1999). Changing the school culture through the instructional program. Interview (Tape on file with authors), October 15.

Redl, F., & Wineman, D. (1952). *Controls from within*. Glencoe, IL: Free Press.

Rest, J. (1979). *Development in judging moral issues*. Minneapolis, MN: University of Minnesota Press.

Schmidt, J. J. (1999). *Counseling in the schools: Essential services and comprehensive programs* (3rd ed.). Boston: Allyn & Bacon.

Senge, P. M. (1990). *The fifth discipline: The art and practice of the learning organization*. New York: Doubleday.

Senge, P. M., Kleiner, A., Roberts, C., Ross, R., Roth, G., & Smith, B. (1999). *The dance of change: The challenges of sustaining momentum in learning organizations*. New York: Doubleday.

Telushkin, J. (1996). *Words that hurt, words that heal*. New York: William Morrow.

Wiggins, G., & McTighe, J. (1998). *Understanding by design*. Alexandria, VA: ASCD.

Williams, M. M. (1993, November). Actions speak louder than words: What students think. *Educational Leadership, 51*, 22–23.

Witkin, B. R. (1984). *Assessing needs in educational and social programs*. San Francisco: Jossey Bass.

Index

Note: Page numbers followed by an *f* indicate a figure.

About the Authors

Rita Prager Stein is a Central Office Administrator for the Half Hollow Hills School District. She received her doctorate from Teachers College, Columbia University; her dissertation focused on the effect of instruction on the moral reasoning of students. She has presented workshops on this topic at Columbia University, New York University, and throughout the country. She is an adjunct professor at Suffolk Community College and has recently published an article in the New England Middle School Journal. Stein does consulting work in districts on a variety of topics. She and her coauthors can be reached at circhcond@aol.com.

Roberta A. Richin is a staff and curriculum development specialist consulting to public and private schools, universities, law enforcement agencies, health services, parent organizations, state education departments, and corporations. Richin brings 25 years of experience to this model for improving student learning, school safety, character, and conduct through curriculum, instruction, and discipline practices. She is an adjunct instructor at The State University of New York at Stony Brook and has published a variety of journal articles and curricula.

Richard Banyon is the Assistant Superintendent for Personnel, Curriculum, and Instruction for the Deer Park School District. He has more than 30 years of experience as a classroom teacher, guidance counselor, dean, building administrator, and central office administrator in New York City and Long Island. He has presented workshops on preparing new teachers for the classroom, including classroom management and instructional strategies.

Francine Banyon is the Assistant Principal for grades 10–12 at the Smithtown Central School District High School. She has 30 years of experience as a dropout prevention coordinator, dean, and building administrator both in New York City and on Long Island. She has presented workshops on peer mediation, conflict resolution, and The Circle of Character and Conduct.

Marc N. Stein was a school psychologist, a professional development consultant, and a professor at The State University of New York Suffolk Community College. In his private practice as a therapist, Stein specialized in working with individuals and families in the area of marriage counseling. He presented workshops to corporations and service organizations on leadership, organizational skills, and communication skills.

Related ASCD Resources: Character and Conduct

ASCD stock numbers are noted in parentheses.

Audiotapes

Character Development Through Cooperative Strategies by Spencer Kagan
(#200178)

Creating a Community with Character by David Archibald (#200071)

*Developing Character Through Emotional and Social Competencies in the Pre-K–12
Curriculum* by Susan Carroll (#297089)

Educating for Character in a New Century by Rushworth Kidder (#200207)

How Not to Teach Values: A Critical Look at Character Education by Alfie Kohn
(#296112)

Print Products

Character Education (*Educational Leadership,* v. 51, n. 3; #611-93175)

Developing a Character Education Program: One School District's Experience by
Henry A. Huffman (#194225)

Talk It Out: Conflict Resolution in the Elementary Classroom by Barbara Porro
(#196018)

*The Soul of Education: Helping Students Find Connection, Compassion, and
Character at School* by Rachael Kessler (#100045)

Videotapes

Character Education: Restoring Respect and Responsibility in Our Schools by
National Professional Resources, Inc. (#396286)

For additional resources, visit us on the World Wide Web (http://www.
ascd. org), send an e-mail message to member@ascd.org, call the ASCD
Service Center (1-800-933-ASCD or 703-578-9600, then press 2),
send a fax to 703-575-5400, or write to Information Services, ASCD,
1703 N. Beauregard St., Alexandria, VA 22311-1714 USA.